Jennifer

T0302473

111 Places in Ottawa That You Must Not Miss

Photographs by Liz Beddall

emons:

Happy travels to the Bain-MacKenzie clan

© Emons Verlag GmbH
All rights reserved
© Photographs by Liz Beddall, except see p. 238
Layout: Eva Kraskes, based on a design
by Lübbeke | Naumann | Thoben
Maps: altancicek.design, www.altancicek.de
Basic cartographical information from Openstreetmap,
© OpenStreetMap-Mitwirkende, OdbL
Editing: Karen E. Seiger
Printing and binding: Grafisches Centrum Cuno, Calbe
Printed in Germany 2022
ISBN 978-3-7408-1388-8
First edition

Guidebooks for Locals & Experienced Travelers
Join us in uncovering new places around the world at
www.111places.com

Foreword

Not many capital cities are as unpretentious or as understated as Canada's. Built where the Ottawa, Rideau and Gatineau Rivers converge, Ottawa draws its name from an Algonquin word meaning "to trade." This is a G7 capital and a bilingual government town packed with embassies and national museums. But it's also a high-tech town with a great wealth of green space, starting with more than 800 kilometres (500 miles) of bike paths. Sure, outsiders from bigger, splashier cities might still call Ottawa staid. But when Ottawans let that tired insult slide off their backs, it seems to me a sly move to keep their unspoiled city to themselves.

Here's the confounding thing about Ottawa, though – it's not really just Ottawa. Quebec and the jewel known as Gatineau Park are just over an inter-provincial bridge, and everyone travels back and forth with ease. In government-speak, the Greater Ottawa-Gatineau Area includes the City of Ottawa in Ontario, the City of Gatineau in Quebec, and the municipalities around each. I'm with those who call everything the "National Capital Region." The population might only be 1.4 million, but here's my favourite fun fact about how much land there is: You can fit five Canadian cities – Toronto, Montreal, Vancouver, Edmonton and Calgary – within the Ottawa city limits.

It has been a minute since my Carleton University journalism years, when I drank at the Laff and danced in Hull but was otherwise oblivious to the city's myriad eccentricities, secrets and wonders. This book is my attempt to rectify that.

The book was conceived, researched, written and photographed during a global pandemic. The fact that you're about to read about 111 compelling places (222 counting the ones found in the "tips") is a testament to everyone featured on these pages, who survived ever-changing rules, restrictions, and closures – not to mention the pandemic itself – and still eagerly made time to share their stories.

111 Places

1 Afrotechture
A space for Black artisans and curators

Housed in the ByWard Market building, alongside food merchants, artisans and specialty boutiques, Afrotechture is a shop that showcases Black creators. "Everything in our store is from the Black diaspora," explains co-founder Resa Solomon-St. Lewis. To counter the misconception that the Black community is, she continues, "a monolith, homogenous, Afrotechture brings together Black Canadians, different parts of the Caribbean and different parts of Africa. We're really excited to share the diversity in our culture."

Afrotechture was created by sisters Resa and Tracey Solomon, who were born in Winnipeg but whose family roots are in Trinidad. Resa trained as a chemical engineer and became chef-owner of Baccanalle Foods, which started in farmers' markets and evolved into a restaurant that now offers Caribbean meal kits. Brooklyn-based Tracey is a business consultant and serial entrepreneur, who owns Flatbush Granola Co.

What started with a pop-up during a holiday fair in 2020 became the 500-square-foot Afrotechture store the following spring. The name combines "afro" (meaning Black) and "techture" as in architecture. The shop has been involved in Afro World Fest and proudly reports that its vividly coloured Dashiki Print Cushion appeared in *Song & Story: Amazing Grace*, an Oprah Winfrey Network movie.

The shop stocks pillows in unique textiles and others with truisms, like "Black Lives Matter." Bath, beauty and body items include Twenty20 Skincare products made with fair-trade shea butter from Ghana. Slip on a kimono made from Ankara fabrics by Akani Designs. African princess dolls, first created by a local artisan to help her daughter build self-esteem, wear beautiful textiles. Take home Baccanalle spice blends, jerk barbecue sauces and cranberry hibiscus compote, along with frozen patties, jerk chicken and curries, plus Eight50 Coffee sourced from Ethiopia.

Address 55 ByWard Market Square, Unit 11, Ottawa, ON K1N 9C3, +1 (343) 574-6297, www.afrotechture.com, info@afrotechture.com | Getting there O-Train to Rideau (Line 1) | Hours Fri–Sun 11am–5pm | Tip The Flava Factory is Ottawa's only street dance studio and teaches popping, breaking, house, locking, hip hop, vogue, waacking and dancehall (1076 Wellington Street W, www.flavafactory.ca).

2 Alanis Private

You oughta know this street

In the suburban Ottawa neighbourhood of Emerald Wood, a dead-end residential street, just steps long and featuring only a handful of townhomes, doesn't seem the most logical place to be named after musician Alanis Morissette. But it's right here that you'll find "Alanis Private."

You probably haven't seen many streets with names that end with the suffix "private" instead of avenue, road or drive. It signifies that this is a private road and that the property owners who included it in their development once submitted an application to name a private road, detailing the name's origin and history and complying with the Commemorative Naming Policy. They paid for and continue to maintain the sign. Whatever the red tape, attaching the word "private" to the singer who suffered post-traumatic stress disorder from her intense *Jagged Little Pill* fame seems fitting.

Morissette, of the 1995 jilted-lover anthem "You Oughta Know" and pop hit "Ironic," has lived in California for decades, but Ottawans proudly claim her as one of their own. Winner of Juno and Grammy awards, the singer-songwriter was born here, moved to Germany for a few years with her teacher parents, and then returned for Catholic school and Glebe Collegiate, while launching her music career as a teen. From 2001 to 2016, she owned an 11th-floor, sub-penthouse condo at 40 Boteler Street in ByWard Market with Ottawa River views. People will point it out to you if you take a boat tour.

There's no public trace of why someone honoured Alanis for what's called on the bilingual "privé Alanis Pvt." street sign, but the Canadian American singer does occasionally reminisce about her roots. "My hometown of Ottawa Ontario Canada will always have a soft place in my heart," Alanis tweeted to promote a musical fundraiser for Shepherds of Good Hope, a soup kitchen where she volunteered as a child.

Address Alanis Private, Ottawa, ON K1T 4A1 | **Getting there** Bus 6, 40, 98 to Hunt Club/Bridle Path or 1145 Hunt Club | **Hours** Unrestricted | **Tip** Fans of *The X-Files* will make a pilgrimage to the corner of Mulder Avenue and Scully Way in a seemingly quiet residential neighbourhood in the city's east end.

3 Algonquin College
Jennifer Lawrence filmed here

In March 2012, Jennifer Lawrence shot to stardom as Katniss Everdeen in the first of four *Hunger Games* films, based on the popular book series by Suzanne Collins. Six months later, a movie she had filmed in Ottawa in 2010 was also released. *House at the End of the Street* is a psychological thriller about teenager Elissa Cassidy, who moves to a woodsy suburb with her divorcée mom Sarah (Elisabeth Shue). She falls for the reclusive Ryan Jacobson (Max Theriot), whose parents were slain by his younger sister. The sister disappeared, and Ryan lives alone in the house / massacre site.

Rotten Tomatoes gave the film just 13 per cent on its Tomatometer, calling it "poorly conceived, clumsily executed, and almost completely bereft of scares." The *Ottawa Sun* was more generous, calling it "a funky slasher film" and urging people to watch for Ottawa's blue-and-white cop cars and to listen for *Jagged Little Pill* by Alanis Morissette (see ch. 2). Nevertheless, true JLaw fans know that much of the filming happened here before she was a star – at Metcalfe and Carp homes and on a Nepean soundstage. Visit the most public filming location, Algonquin College, which stood in as Woodshire High School, and see the iconic exterior of "P Building," aka the Police & Public Safety Institute.

Attracting film and TV projects is the Ottawa Film Office's job. You can go on their eight self-guided film tours that focus on Little Italy, Centretown, Orléans and Rural Ottawa East, Rural Ottawa South, Hintonburg, Vanier, the Glebe and ByWard Market. The city has a burgeoning reputation for Christmas films too, which only makes sense, given that snow is all but guaranteed for winter fimling. But it isn't the snow that attracts films like *Boyfriends of Christmas Past*, *Christmas CEO* and *Candy Cane Candidate* – it's the "historic buildings, romantic courtyards, charming small towns, and an assortment of film-friendly businesses," according to the Film Office's website.

Address 1385 Woodroffe Avenue, Ottawa, ON K2G 1V8, +1 (613) 727-4723, www.algonquincollege.com | Getting there Bus 88 to Algonquin College / College | Hours Unrestricted | Tip In the 2014 mockumentary *Trailer Park Boys: Don't Legalize It*, the character Ricky went to the lawn of Parliament Hill to protest the potential legalization of marijuana that might kill his grow op (111 Wellington Street).

4 Andaz Rooftop Lounge
Sunsets from a great height

Ottawa is a city that likes to pause and worship its sunsets. People will gather at the end of the day on patios and beaches, on blankets and in lawn chairs, along the river and canal. And those who crave loftier views with creature comfort are drawn to Copper Spirits & Sights, the city's tallest indoor/outdoor rooftop lounge on the 16th floor of the Andaz Ottawa ByWard Market hotel. The westward-facing view takes in the ByWard Market, downtown core and copper-topped Parliament buildings – no sunset needed. A couple of tables even offer northward views of the Ottawa River and Quebec's Gatineau Hills.

Fireworks viewing is another draw. The patio boasts views of the country's most epic display of Canada Day fireworks and more for New Year's Eve. Every Wednesday and Saturday in August, you can even see the light shows from Casino Lac-Leamy in Gatineau. There are craft cocktails, craft beer and small plates to be had, and the Copper Mule and Espresso Martini are two favourites. Whisky and gin are barrel-aged on site.

The 90-seat patio isn't staffed in winter, although you can ask to step outside with your drink. But the Andaz does transform its patio into "Copper on Ice" during the three weekends of Winterlude, with an ice bar, vodka drink luge, firepits, blankets and winter-themed cocktails. There might even be cocoa and maple taffy, which is made by pouring boiling Canadian maple syrup on snow and twirling it onto a popsicle stick.

When the 200-room Andaz opened in 2016, it was the first for the brand, which is part of Hyatt Hotels, in Canada. Interior design firm Mason Studio made each of the 16 storeys reflect "the history and character of a Canadian province or territory." Artwork has been curated by the Canada Council Art Bank. The hotel restaurant, Feast + Revel, offers New Canadian ingredient-driven dishes, such as Peameal Eggs Benedict, and fish and chips made with pickerel.

Address 325 Dalhousie Street, Ottawa, ON K1N 7G1, +1 (613) 321-1234, www.hyatt.com, ottawa.guest@andaz.com | Getting there O-Train to Rideau (Line 1) | Hours Sun & Wed–Thu 6–10pm, Fri & Sat 5–11pm | Tip From the Mackenzie King Bridge, ponder the Shaw Centre, a curved glass convention centre that was designed to resemble a large tulip lying on its side (55 Colonel By Drive, www.shaw-centre.com).

5 Annie Pootoogook Park

Honouring an Inuk artist

To celebrate International Inuit Day on November 7, 2021, Canada's first Inuk Governor-General Mary Simon, throat singers, drum dancers and other Ottawans gathered to see a downtown park renamed after the late, acclaimed Inuk artist Annie Pootoogook. The third-generation artist was born in Kinngait (formerly Cape Dorset), Nunavut and later lived in Ottawa until she died in September 2016 at the age of 47, leaving behind daughter Napachie and a legion of people who loved her pen and coloured pencil drawings of contemporary Inuit life. In festivities that included a country food feast with seal, Arctic char, Arctic berries and bannock, the Governor-General praised the way that Annie Pootoogook captured the Inuit way of life with art that depicted everything from hunting, community feasts and bannock-making to shopping, watching TV and domestic violence.

In 2006, Annie Pootoogook won the $50,000 Sobey Art Award. At times, galleries sold her drawings for thousands of dollars. Her most famous piece, *Dr. Phil*, shows an Inuk girl lying on the floor watching the American talk show. But after moving to Ottawa in 2007, she struggled with addiction and mental health challenges, lived in homeless shelters and parks and sometimes sold her art on the street. Her body was found in the Rideau River near Bordeleau Park. While police investigated the death as suspicious, no arrests were made. An officer who posted racist comments online pleaded guilty to discreditable conduct and underwent sensitivity training.

Annie Pootoogook Park, behind the Sandy Hill Community Centre, was spearheaded by area resident Stéphanie Plante. Kids enjoy the play structures, a wading pool, seasonal rink and ping pong table. The adjoining community centre that displays art from three Inuit artists from the city's collection, including Annie's *Late Night Snack* and *Composition (Listening to the Radio with Coffee)*.

Address Behind the Sandy Hill Community Centre, 250 Somerset Street East, Ottawa, ON K1N 6V6, +1 (613) 564-1062, 311@ottawa.ca | **Getting there** O-Train to uOttawa (Line 1) | **Hours** Unrestricted | **Tip** Barely Bruised Books is known for its large outdoor Little Free Library. Indigenous owner Scott MacKillop stocks many Indigenous authors (315 Wilbrod Street, second floor, www.ottawabookstore.ca).

6 Anti-Poverty Monument
Honouring activist Dorothy O'Connell

On Ottawa City Hall's south lawn, you might spot someone perched in a house-shaped nook carved out of a piece of red granite that resembles a giant slice of bread. On the interior wall, a quote by the late activist/playwright Dorothy O'Connell reads, *Poverty stops equality. Equality stops poverty.* This is the *Dorothy O'Connell Monument to Anti-Poverty Activism* by local multimedia artist and cultural researcher cj fleury to honour the Ottawan who was called "the poet laureate of the poor."

The monument expresses the struggle that many people face to buy food or pay the rent. "Anti-poverty activism, an intimidating issue, was made approachable through this portrayal and gave dignity to the impoverished," explains the artist on her website. Fleury believes the "somewhat humorous form" of the monument invites people to come closer and contemplate the artwork's meaning. The monument was unveiled October 17, 2004, to mark the United Nations' International Day for the Eradication of Poverty. O'Connell, mother of five, died May 22, 2020, at the age of 80.

Dorothy O'Connell laced her activism with humour. She wrote *Chiclet Gomez* and *Cock-Eyed Optimists*, books of short stories based on her family's life in public housing, mainly in the Rochester Heights community housing neighbourhood. Gomez (O'Connell's alter ego) had adventures with characters named Tillie, King Kong, Fat Freddie and Housing Authority bureaucrats.

O'Connell was known for holding social events, and she also launched a tenant organization for housing issues. She was involved in the city's first community legal clinic and co-founded the Ottawa Women's Credit Union, providing services for women to establish their own financial independence. She made a fundraising button that stated, "Pierre Trudeau lives in Public Housing," and famously got the prime minister at the time to wear it to the House of Commons.

POVERTY
STOPS
EQUALITY

EQUALITY
STOPS
POVERTY

O' O'CONNELL

Address South Lawn, Ottawa City Hall, 110 Laurier Avenue West, Ottawa, ON K1P 1J1, +1 (613) 580-2400 or 311, www.ottawa.ca | Getting there O-Train to Parliament (Line 1) | Hours Unrestricted | Tip Fans can share a moment with a bronze of Canadian jazz legend Oscar Peterson, who is seated at a piano with room on the bench beside him outside the National Arts Centre (Elgin and Albert Streets, www.nac-cna.ca).

7 Art House Café
Where art is for everyone

The dream for Art House Café was for it to be a hub for artists and non-artists to meet around art. When it launched in 2017, Geneviève Bétournay remembers, there weren't enough opportunities in the city to showcase local artists or to help them find resources to develop new skills and meet like-minded people. Fast forward to now, and the café, nestled into the main floor of a 150-year-old house, is "filled as much as we possibly can with art, while also leaving it as a functional space," says Bétournay.

Bétournay, who started as art director and took over as owner in 2019, usually hangs 250-odd pieces from 100 different local and regional artists and showcases more items, like felted creations, soaps, t-shirts and prints, in the gift shop. "I wanted to bring art to the masses," she explains. "I wanted to sell art to the 95 per cent that don't even realize that art is meaningful to them. I didn't want to sell art to the five per cent who already buy art and walk into galleries."

Sometimes several pieces by one artist might be grouped in one spot, but typically they're scattered through the rooms, treasure-hunt style. Most are priced in the $25 to $300 range, but a few come in over $1,000. The café takes a 30 per cent commission (lower than galleries) and doesn't demand exclusivity. A diversity of styles, sizes, mediums and content is essential. This individuality, Bétournay believes, "makes people feel better about who they are – and being unique and being weird and whatever they are."

The café itself revolves around creative hot drinks, like the surprise latte of the day, and cocktails, and extends to sandwiches and soups. "Fancy" grilled cheeses are popular. At night, the vibe is bar-lounge. If there isn't an event, concert, workshop or meetup happening, you'll likely find artists doing their own thing, be it visual arts, writing or playing the piano.

Address 555 Somerset Street W, Ottawa, ON K1R 5K1, +1 (613) 518-4782, www.thearthousecafe.ca, info@thearthousecafe.ca | Getting there O-Train to Lyon (Line 1), then a 10-minute walk | Hours Mon–Thu 10am–10pm, Fri & Sat 10am–midnight, Sun 10am–9pm | Tip Darling Vintage offers clothes plus vintage wedding gowns for the "less-fussy, eco-friendly and cost-conscious bride" (502 Somerset Street W, www.instagram.com/darlingvintageshop).

8 _ Art-Is-In Bakery
Home of Ottawa's signature pastry

Ottawans call the city O-Town, so it's fitting that Art-Is-In Bakery makes a decadent, O-shaped pastry called the O-Towner.

"The process is like a croissant, but the dough is like a donut," explains co-owner Stéphanie Mathieson. Her pastry chef husband Kevin takes laminated donut dough, cuts out rounds that are about 100 layers each, and deep-fries them in a blend of palm and coconut oil. He rolls the puffed, crusty-on-the outside layered donuts in cinnamon sugar, inserts a paring knife in three spots in the bottom, and pipes in flavoured pastry cream. Pistachio is popular, but you can try flavours from raspberry and coffee to vanilla caramel, apple caramel and chocolate brownie. The tops are decorated with more colourful pastry cream and tiny, crunchy wafer balls. O-Towners, which Kevin started making in 2014, are similar to the iconic Cronuts invented by French American pastry chef Dominique Ansel. O-Towners started out as Kronuts (with a K for Kevin) before settling on their name.

Art-Is-In sells about 500 O-Towners a week, but the gastro-bakery has a lot more to offer than just one pastry. Kevin was classically trained in New York and Europe, falling in love with pastries first and then bread before returning to Ottawa. Art-Is-In launched for wholesale in 2006 in a small, back-lane space before moving to the City Centre complex in 2010 – before it was a destination – and embracing retail.

As for the bakery's name, Stéphanie says, "Creating art is so important to Kevin. It's part of his life. So, he just came up with this Art-Is-In, which also sounds like 'artisan.' Everything is handcrafted."

There's room for 105 people inside and 60 on the patio. Regulars come for the pastries and bread, but also daily brunch (think *croque monsieur*) and sourdough pizza (think Hipster Pepperoni and Vegan Veggie). And if the O-Towner is too much, there's always O-Towner Holes.

Address 250 City Centre Avenue, Unit 112, Ottawa, ON K1R 6K7, +1 (613) 695-1226 ext. 1, www.artisinbakery.com, admin@artisinbakery.com | Getting there O-Train to Bayview (Line 1) | Hours Tue–Sat 9am–7pm, Fri 9am–8pm, Sun 9am–2pm | Tip Beyond the Pale Brewing Company has a stellar patio, BTP Smoquehouse. It isn't all meat, so try cauliflower wings and smoked and dusted tofu (250 City Centre, Unit 108, www.bbtpshop.ca).

9 Au Feel de L'eau

Hail a water taxi for a river crossing

Among the crowded tour boats that ply the Ottawa River is Au feel de L'eau, a tiny and eco-friendly water taxi. Hop aboard and travel slowly and quietly between Gatineau and Ottawa.

These water taxis glide without engine noise or exhaust fumes. When Sylvie Lyonnais and Jean-Marc Hénot launched the business in 2011, being environmentally friendly was a priority. Hénot designed two pontoon boats and had them custom made locally. One yellow and one burgundy, the boats (29- and 30-footers) can carry 12 passengers, as well as wheelchairs, bikes and strollers. They're powered by electric motors with lithium-ion batteries that can run for 12 hours and plug into shore power to recharge at night. Solar panels on the roof of the boats charge service batteries for radios and lights.

The couple are avid sailors who moved here and immediately realized that people who don't own boats can't enjoy the river as much from the shore. They were inspired to see electric pedal boats in Quebec that are quiet enough to approach even skittish loons. Lyonnais says the business' name reflects the feeling you get "when you're on the water taxi and you really feel the water."

The water taxis zip between provinces on an endless loop of journeys, generally under 10 minutes long. Short Trips are the routes between Gatineau's Canadian Museum of History, the wharf at the foot of the Ottawa locks and Richmond Landing near the Canadian War Museum (see ch. 70), offering views of Parliament Hill and its staircase through the trees (see ch. 79). The longer Resto Bar Loop is by reservation and takes you between Ottawa's Rockcliffe boathouse and Gatineau's Rest'O'Bord Le Pirate restaurant dock, with the chance to get off and linger at each spot. You can also book private, 90-minute outings on the Aqua Limo for special occasions, like the fireworks on Canada Day and the fireworks festival at Casino du Lac Leamy.

Address See website for landing locations, +1 (819) 329-2413, www.aquataxi.ca, info@aufeeldeleau.ca | Getting there Varies by location | Hours Mid-May–Sep daily 11am–7pm, Sep–Oct daily 11am–6pm | Tip Ottawa Boat Cruise/Croisières Outaouais has an all-electric tour boat that was built in Gatineau for seasonal Rideau Canal cruises (departs 1 Elgin Street, below Plaza Bridge, www.ottawaboatcruise.com).

10 Barbie Museum
Stittsville flea market celebrates dolls

It's tough to find a good, old-school flea market these days, with free parking and the unmistakable smell of vintage furniture and used books. Luckily, the flea in Stittsville offers all of that, and it's also quietly home to the Barbie Museum.

Stittsville's Carp Road Flea Market has been going strong since 2005, drawing an eclectic mix of indoor/outdoor vendors proffering collectibles, jewelry, jams, fudge, lawn mowers, tools, records, beer glasses, golf clubs and everything in between, including Red Rose Tea's miniature ceramic figures. A family business oversees the flea market and Kondruss Galleries, an antique showroom that specializes in dining and bedroom suites.

Elizabeth Kondruss doubles as the Barbie Museum's founder and curator. She fell in love with the iconic Barbie doll (debuted March 9, 1959) as a nine-year-old child and has been collecting ever since. There once was a time when you bought dolls and clothes separately, but now Barbie comes clothed to suit her profession, be it a rock star, astronaut or veterinarian. Kondruss figures she has one of the largest collections in the world – and she makes it clear that she isn't associated with the Mattel Corporation.

Some inexpensive dolls have a prominent space on shelves just inside the front door, but at the east side of the building, beside the Kondruss Galleries area, is a larger "museum" space for glass cabinets packed with Barbie treasures, including clothing created by fashion designer and icon Bob Mackie.

Kondruss has more than 24,000 pieces in her collection, including clothes, houses, bikes, horses, furniture and cars, but she only has room to display about a quarter of it. Everything is insured. She sells dolls for which she has duplicates. Some items are priced for the average person (like $3 dolls), while others are for serious collectors. She also does restorations and appraisals.

Address 2079 Carp Road, Stittsville, ON K0A 1L0, +1 (613) 836-3103, www.carprdfleamarket.net, carprdfleamarket@gmail.com | Getting there Bus 262, 303 to Carp/Lloydalex | Hours Flea Market Sun 9am–5pm, Gallery Wed & Sat 10am–4pm | Tip Pretty Pots Flower Shop is in an old general store/bank. An old walk-in bank safe is now a flower cooler and a vintage punch clock (1528 Stittsville Main Street, Stittsville, www.prettypotsflowers.com).

11 Bate Island

Mecca for surfers, kayakers and birders

Surfers and kayakers know this tiny, urban island on the Ottawa River just off the Champlain Bridge as a place where they can frolic in a handful of waves, especially in the spring, when the snow melts and the water level and flow rate are ideal. Surfers have even gathered here for landlocked Surf Jams. Kayakers gravitate here all summer.

Bate Island also draws picnickers, sunset seekers and birders. Signs implore you to not feed the birds, namely the noisy, aggressive Canada geese, even if they have cute offspring in tow. Per one such sign, one of the five reasons to keep wildlife wild is because feeding the birds "may affect water quality, due to their excrement." On the south side of the island, you may spot people looking westward, with their binoculars trained on the water. They are looking at an Important Bird Area (IBA), with gulls year-round, aerial insectivores during migration and waterfowl during migration and wintertime.

Five Nature Canada interpretation signs tell you what you need to know about IBAs, like the fact they host "threatened species, endemic species, species representative of a biome or highly exceptional concentration of birds." IBAs are strategic building blocks for global conservation. "For birds, they are literally the most important places on Earth." This part of the river is a wildlife superhighway that sees thousands of waterfowl and waterbirds congregate each spring and fall as they migrate between Ontario / Quebec and warmer climates to the South. Songbirds use the river and the forests along the banks for food and shelter.

More than 300 bird species have been spotted here – everything from harlequin ducks and Barrow's goldeneye to peregrine falcons, common nighthawks, chimney swifts, barn swallows and red-headed woodpeckers. Serious birders don't usually acknowledge the Canada goose, but some secretly admire it.

Address Access via the Champlain Bridge (Island Park Drive) | Getting there O-Train to Tunney's Pasture (Line 1), transfer to bus 16 to Clearview/Island Park, then walk 15 minutes | Hours Unrestricted | Tip *Pangishimo* means "sunset" in Algonquin, and this park highlights Indigenous culture and heritage in a natural-style public green space (western shore of Chaudières Island, www.ncc-ccn.gc.ca).

12 BeaverTails
Mouthful of Canadiana

Beavers are an emblem of Canada. In a fun twist, a deep-fried pastry shaped like and named for a beaver tail – the industrious mammal's rudder for swimming – has become an iconic dessert associated with skating. The BeaverTails pastry starts with a yeasted whole wheat/cracked wheat dough that's hand-stretched into large, flat ovals, then deep-fried to order, sprinkled with cinnamon and sugar (at the very least) and handed to you piping hot with crispy edges. "Canada's pastry" is best eaten as you skate down the Rideau Canal.

Grant and Pam Hooker started serving BeaverTails for 75 cents apiece at the Killaloe Craft and Community Fair in the Ottawa Valley in 1978, based on a family recipe for *küchle*, and then brought them to the ByWard Market and the Rideau Canal. "It's a new version of an old traditional food item that was present in early Canada and has similar cousins around the world," says Grant. "We came up with the name simply because that is the appearance. It was one of the best decisions we could ever have made because it linked our food to Canada."

In 1987, Pino Di loia joined the Hookers when he was a university student. He is now majority owner, along with his wife and twin brother, of BeaverTails, a company that has been name-checked on *Jeopardy* and *South Park*. The Hookers maintain 35 per cent ownership and exclusive rights to the National Capital Region territory.

Grant built the year-round ByWard Market stall himself in 1980, and in 2009 US President Barack Obama paid them a visit. Chocolate hazelnut spread is a fan favourite. Purists swear by the Classic, sprinkled with cinnamon and sugar, and the Killaloe Sunrise adds a slice of lemon to those basic sweeteners for a DIY squeezing experience with a tart twist. On the savoury front, there are Beaverdogs, hot dogs wrapped in the fried pastry, and Poutails, poutine served on a BeaverTails pastry.

Address 69 George Street, Ottawa, ON K1N 1K1, +1 (613) 241-1230, www.beavertails.com, ottawabywardmarket@beavertails.com | **Getting there** O-Train to Rideau (Line 1) | **Hours** Sun–Thu 11am–10pm, Fri 11am–11pm | **Tip** Putting bacon on its maple doughnut has been a hit for SuzyQ Doughnuts, which riffs off a traditional Finnish munkki recipe from the owner's family (1015 Wellington Street W, www.suzyq.ca).

13 Beechwood Cemetery
Making reconciliation efforts

Not far from the entrance of Beechwood Cemetery, a once-over-looked grave is finally getting the attention it deserves. It belongs to Dr. Peter Henderson Bryce (1853–1932), a public health pioneer who raised the alarm about the horrific health abuses and high death rates facing Indigenous children in the residential school system.

While he was the federal immigration department's chief medical officer, Bryce was asked by the Department of Indian Affairs to report on health conditions in residential schools in western Canada. He discovered unsanitary conditions, inadequate medical care and improperly counted deaths, and he demanded improved national policies. Bryce was soon forced to retire from the civil service and self-publish his report, *The Story of a National Crime: Being a Record of the Health Conditions of the Indians of Canada from 1904 to 1921.*

Canada's National Cemetery has collaborated with the Indigenous community to create a Reconciling History walk that explains how Canada, from 1831 to 1996, removed more than 150,000 Indigenous children from their homes and sent them to church-run residential schools. *Thousands died of disease, neglect, or mishap*, reads a plaque. *Many suffered physical, spiritual and sexual abuse.* The Truth and Reconciliation Commission's 2015 report called the schools "cultural genocide." Hundreds of unmarked graves are now being found using ground-penetrating radar.

Beechwood, a National Historic Site, now strives to show both the achievements and failings of prominent Canadians who were involved with the Indigenous community. A plaque for Duncan Campbell Scott, a Confederation poet, has been amended to reveal that he oversaw the residential school system and wanted *to get rid of the Indian problem*. But Bryce's grave is now marked by extra flowers, thank you cards and small markers with "Every Child Matters" slogans.

Address 280 Beechwood Avenue, Vanier, ON K1L 8A6, +1 (613) 741-9530, www.beechwoodottawa.ca, info@beechwoodottawa.ca | Getting there Bus 7 to Beechwood/Juliana | Hours Daily dawn–dusk | Tip Artist/portrait photographer Yousuf Karsh is buried at Notre-Dame Cemetery, Ottawa's oldest and largest Catholic cemetery (455 Montreal Road, www.notredamecemetery.ca).

14 Bison and Moose Dioramas

Canadian Museum of Nature's art behind the scenes

A bison stands in snow laced with prairie grass, with his head down and curved horns pointed towards two wolves. Behind him is a painted scene showing his herd foraging through the snow, oblivious to the threat. This diorama is one of 16 in the Canadian Museum of Nature's Mammal Gallery that offers realistic, three-dimensional recreations of wildlife habitats, this one being Lake Claire in Wood Buffalo National Park. Another diorama shows a moose in Fundy National Park in New Brunswick. You may remember them from a school field trip, but it's worth paying another visit today.

Backdrops to these two dioramas and six others were painted by the late Manitoba wildlife artist Clarence Tillenius in the 1960s and 1970s. The rest were done by Hugh Monahan and Pat Haldorsen. The dioramas combine iconic Canadian animals preserved and posed by a taxidermist, real and recreated flora and painted landscapes. Each represents a real place, so a grizzly is seen in Waterton Lakes National Park, a muskox in Nunavut and pronghorn in Saskatchewan. Tillenius travelled to study the animals, collect plants and make sketches before planning his dioramas.

The bison and wolves, initially taxidermied by James L. Clark, were later repaired and restored by Terry Morgan. Between 2004 and 2010, the dioramas were cleaned, reassembled and retouched during the museum's renovation. Each now has interactive content on a touch-screen computer.

Museum conservator Lucie Cipera says people are slowly coming to appreciate the way that artists worked closely with scientists for these vintage dioramas to show animals in nature, especially in national parks. "It's like a snapshot of nature. Each diorama has an exact location at a time when there was no travel and no colour TV. It was a way that people could travel the country by going to museums. It inspired people to learn biodiversity."

Address 240 McLeod Street, Ottawa, ON K2P 2R1, +1 (613) 566-4700, www.nature.ca, questions@nature.ca | Getting there Bus 14 to Gladstone/Metcalfe | Hours See website for seasonal hours | Tip Private sloth encounters are a highlight at Little Ray's Nature Centre, Canada's largest exotic animal rescue and home to educational presentations (2781 Colonial Road, www.littlerays.org).

15 Brasseurs du Temps

Beer museum housed in a microbrewery

You might expect a beer "museum" inside a microbrewery / restaurant to be a token undertaking. Not so at Les Brasseurs du Temps (BDT). In glass cases along both sides of a long and winding ramp going down from the ground floor, the displays are thoughtfully packed with storyboards, artefacts, memorabilia and archival photos that trace beer from 4,000 B.C., when it was called "sikaru" and considered a food, through the rise and fall of major breweries and Prohibition to the advent of microbreweries and modern times.

This is Gatineau, so there is much to say about Quebec's brewing history, like the fact that the first commercial brewery was founded in 1668 by Jean Talon. But before that, Marie Rollet, wife of colonist Louis Hébert, was considered the "first brewster in New France." French Canadians traditionally brewed beer at home, at least until the British Army arrived and demanded molasses to make two quarts of beer for each man every day beginning in 1759. Philemon Wright, who founded Hull, arrived in 1800 and soon opened a distillery-brewery "Wrightown." His family owned two breweries. The one in an area called Brewery Creek, beside an Ottawa River inlet, dates back to the early 1800s and is now BDT.

The museum's collection includes a malt kiln thermometer (circa 1890), an English copper malt scoop (circa 1900) and an 18th-century wooden tavern tankard. There are 19th-century German-style growlers used to carry fresh beer home and a pre-Confederation C. Berry Hop Beer jug, plus bottles in a wide range of shapes and colours from countless breweries. It's worth noting that during Prohibition, beginning in 1915, Hull became a portal for smuggling alcohol between Quebec and Ontario and became known as Canada's "Little Chicago." BDT serves pub fare (poutine, beer barbecue ribs) with a French twist (French onion soup made with its own stout, tarte tatin), all with beer pairing ideas.

Address 170 Rue Montcalm, Gatineau, QC J8X 2M2, +1 (819) 205-4999, www.brasseursdutemps.com | Getting there Bus 20, 35, 38 to Montcalm/Gagnon | Hours Tue 5–11pm, Wed–Sat noon–11pm | Tip Théâtre de L'Île was built in 1886 as a water tower and then became Quebec's first municipal theatre (1 Wellington Street, Gatineau, www.gatineau.ca).

16 Bytown Fire Brigade Museum

Preserving firefighting history

Tucked into a suburban strip mall is a unique museum lovingly run by a non-profit historical society. Since 1983, the Bytown Fire Brigade has been preserving the fire heritage and history in Canada's Capital Region. Its museum, which once drew thousands of visitors when it was centrally located in an old fire station in the ByWard Market, now receives just a few visitors at its "condominium warehouse" space.

Let one of the members, perhaps society treasurer Henry Vanwyk, show you around the one-room museum. One highlight is part of a sliding pole from a fire station, although, for insurance purposes, it doesn't go through the floor and connect to downstairs. Another thing you'll enjoy is a collection of vintage, grenade-style glass fire extinguisher "bombs" that were once put up in kitchens and filled with a fire suppression chemical called carbon tetrachloride. The walls are filled with archival photos and stories about historical Ottawa fires, including the one that destroyed the original Parliament building in 1916. And there are also fire helmets from around the world, vintage extinguishers and other artefacts.

Downstairs is a workshop, where volunteers tinker away on vintage vehicles, and a room crammed with about a dozen antique fire trucks and vehicles dating back to the 1800s. The showpiece is an 1886 horse drawn Silsby Steam Pumper. There's a 1922 Model T Chemical Car and an 1850 hand pump. To finance its restoration work, the brigade makes the venue available for special events, including unique weddings, parades, parties and charity fundraisers.

Throughout time, the call of 'fire' has meant responding to a condition that is always dangerous, reads a typed sign on the wall. *In smoke and flame, sacrifices are made to save lives and property. This museum is dedicated to the bravery of those who fight fires.*

Address Unit 1, 2880 Sheffield Road, Ottawa, ON K1B 1A4, +1 (613) 744-0595, www.bytownfire.ca, info@bytownfire.ca | **Getting there** Bus 47 to Walkley / Lancaster (Stop 7291), then walk 10 minutes | **Hours** By appointment | **Tip** The Canadian Firefighters Memorial features a bronze firefighter who has returned to Earth from heaven via a pole to point out names of fallen comrades on a memorial wall (200 Lett Street, www.cfff.ca).

17 Bytown Museum

A politician's "death hand"

The delightfully macabre Victorians loved to have plaster or wax "death masks" made after a loved one died to remember them by or to have a likeness available to create future portraits or statues. For those whose faces were disfigured in death, a hand cast was the traditional substitute. Such was the case when politician Thomas D'Arcy McGee was shot in the back of the head on April 7, 1868, as his landlady, Mrs. Totter, was unlocking the door from the inside of his boarding house at 71 Sparks Street to let him inside.

Born in Ireland, McGee became an Ottawa politician and one of the country's Fathers of Confederation. He spoke out against the Fenian Brotherhood, a revolutionary nationalist organization among the Irish in the United States and Ireland. On that spring morning, when Canada was not quite one year old and McGee's popularity was fading, he was killed at the age of 42. Irish-born tailor Patrick James Whelan, suspected of being a Fenian, was quickly arrested and convicted of murder. Swearing his innocence, he was hanged on February 11, 1869, before thousands of people in one of Canada's last public hangings. The *Canadian Encyclopedia* calls the case "the greatest murder mystery in Canadian political history."

The Bytown Museum acquired the original 1868 white plaster "death hand" of McGee in 1920 through a private donation. Find it on the third floor among Canadian political history artifacts – it's McGee's right hand. "Some may describe this as a fitting tribute for a renowned writer, publisher and orator," collections and exhibitions manager Grant Vogl says. "McGee's writings certainly left an indelible mark on the nation." The museum has made replicas for the Carlingford Heritage Centre in Ireland where McGee was born, and for the D'Arcy McGee's pub at 44 Sparks Street. The museum is housed in the 1827 Commissariat, Ottawa's oldest stone building.

Address 1 Canal Lane, Ottawa, ON K1P 5P6, +1 (613) 234-4570, www.bytownmuseum.com, info@bytownmuseum.ca | Getting there O-Train to Rideau (Line 1) | Hours See website | Tip Dinner, drinks and a show are the package deal at Absolute Comedy, where you can also hire a comedian for your own private party (412 Preston Street, www.absolutecomedy.ca).

18 ByWard Market Bell
Ring a piece of history

Unless you have to use the loo or know about Gallery 55, you may not climb up from a floor of food merchants, boutiques and artisans to the mezzanine level of the ByWard Market building. But it's here that a gorgeous bronze bell hangs inside a wood-panelled skylight, hoping to be rung by locals and visitors.

This bell was cast in 1877 by the Meneely Foundry of West Troy, New York and installed in the original market building, constructed in 1876 and burnt in 1926, reads a plaque. Fortunately, the bell was saved, cleaned, and placed in St. David's R. E. Church. The Northgrave family donated the bell to the City of Ottawa in 1976.

Beyond these scant details, the story is murky. The ByWard Market, established in 1826 by Rideau Canal builder Lieutenant-Colonel John By, is one of Canada's oldest and largest public markets and has indoor/outdoor vendors. The bell once let merchants know exactly when to start and end the workday. When a previous market building was destroyed by fire, the treasured bell was safely relocated to a New Edinburgh church. The church changed hands several times until Brian Northgrave bought it, renovated it for his family and donated the bell to the city in 1976.

The bell was installed in the fifth and current incarnation of the market building but then the bell stopped ringing for no known reason in the 1990s and faded into obscurity. Ottawa historian and artist Andrew King asked the mayor for help in 2018, tweeting, "It's hidden away but can we get this ringing again?" Soon after, the bell got its voice back. The bronze beauty was inspected, insured and given a new rope. Anyone can now call or email the market to set up a time to ring the bell and be photographed with it. "For Whom The Bell Tolls?" tweeted a triumphant King. "YOU." Zach Dayler, Executive Director of Ottawa Markets, says, "This is a robust bell." It's very loud indeed – you can't miss it when it's rung.

Address 55 ByWard Market Square, Ottawa, ON K1N 9C3, www.ottawamarkets.ca/byward-market, +1 (613) 244-4410, info@ottawamarkets.ca | Getting there O-Train to Rideau (Line 1) | Hours See website for seasonal hours | Tip Koven is a heavy metal eatery with a medieval gate to its patio and "morbid cocktails," like Absent God and Possessed Mary (93 Murray Street, www.thekoven.ca).

19   Canada Agriculture & Food Museum

New life for old manure

While the biggest draw at the Canada Agriculture and Food Museum is the cows, pigs, sheep, goats, alpacas, chickens and rabbits, it's fair to say that the impressive manure pile is what will capture your attention. *Today's manure is tomorrow's harvest*, a nearby sign says. *Farmers spread manure over their fields to enrich the soil, and so does the Museum!*

Manure triumphs over synthetic soil because it contains organic matter, improves soil stability, reduces erosion and retains water like a sponge. The particular pile of educational manure at the museum, part of the Central Experimental Farm, is shovelled daily into a trailer and soon transferred to a site with a storage and composting area before it gets spread on fields with specialized machines. To explore the barns here, you must step on blue mats to disinfect your shoes with a non-toxic and biodegradable product because bacteria can hide in farm animal poop, and dirty footwear can spread diseases that might make both people and animals quite sick.

Look for the photo quiz that shows five poops and guess which animal is responsible for each one. The tiny pellet is high in potassium and great for pumpkin and potatoes, while a goopy glob is low in nutrients but great for improving soil structure.

This 400-hectare farm was established in 1886 as the central research station for Canada's Department of Agriculture and is the world's only working farm in a capital city. The museum part of things includes a horse and cattle barn, poultry house, small animal barn, learning centre that explores food preservation (complete with a root cellar), soil lab, dairy barn and a canola exhibition. There's also a discovery park and demonstration kitchen. Children are welcome here.

Address 901 Prince of Wales Drive, Ottawa, ON K2C 3K1, +1 (613) 991-3044, www.ingeniumcanada.org/agriculture, contact@ingeniumcanada.org | Getting there O-Train to Carleton (Line 1), then walk 10 minutes | Hours Wed–Sun 9am–5pm | Tip Chef Ric's is a social enterprise for the Ottawa Mission. Chef Ric Watson sells affordable prepared meals, runs a catering company and a mobile food truck (384 Rideau Street, www.chefrics.com).

20 Carbide Willson Ruins
Hike to see industrial heritage

Thomas Leopold "Carbide" Willson was a prolific inventor and electrochemistry pioneer who earned his nickname by developing technology in 1892 to mass produce calcium carbide. When calcium carbide pellets are dampened with water, they produce extremely flammable acetylene gas, which burns with a bright white light. It was once prized for domestic and industrial lighting.

Although he invented it in the United States, the Ontario-born Willson soon decamped to Ottawa. Besides being credited as the first Ottawan to own an automobile, the wealthy industrialist built a summer house on 400-odd acres of land at Meech Lake in the Gatineau Hills in 1907. Four years later, he built an acid condensation tower, dam and generating station as an experimental fertilizer plant where Meech Creek meets Little Meech Lake. Willson House is now a classified federal heritage building used for small conferences.

Willson isn't well known, but the story of his achievements does circulate with those who visit the spectacular Carbide Willson Ruins. The ruins are hidden in a forest about a 30-minute hike from the closest National Capital Commission (NCC) parking lot. Fire swept through the tower, so only the foundation remains. "The dam and plant, its gaping windows still visible, stand near the cascading falls as a reminder of a rich and innovative company – and a glimpse of our scientific history," writes the NCC on its website. At the site, a fading interpretation sign states, *Within these walls, now in ruins, [Willson] condensed phosphoric acid to produce phosphate fertilizer.*

Willson, who registered more than 70 patents, raised the ire of waterfront cottagers with experiments that tampered with water levels. He lost his fortune when he took out loans with a single investor and missed a payment. He died of a heart attack in 1915 while in New York trying to hustle venture capital.

Address Gatineau Park, Trail 36 from parking lot P11 (O'Brien Beach), Chemin du Lac-Meech, Chelsea, QC J9B 1H9, +1 (613) 239-5000, www.ncc-ccn.gc.ca/places/carbide-willson-ruins, info@ncc-ccn.ca | Getting there By car, take Autoroute de la Gatineau (A-5), take exit 13 to Chemin Old Chelsea, then Chemin du Lac Meech to the trailhead | Hours See website for seasonal hours | Tip La Petite Grocerie is a gift shop full of local products made by Quebec artisans and food producers (244 Old Chelsea Road, Chelsea, www.facebook.com / Lagroceriechelsea).

21　Cedars & Co.
Shawarma in a supermarket setting

When you walk into Cedars & Co., you're enveloped in intoxicating aromas. There's meat being grilled, sweet and savoury spices, a hint of orange and a whiff of *toum*, Lebanon's fluffy, white garlic sauce. In the food market's front corner, you'll see a shawarma counter, where marinated pieces of chicken and beef have been piled onto a vertical revolving spit. The meat will be carved to order for plates, platters or sandwiches and served with your desired mix of pickled turnips, hummus, tabbouleh, tahini, garlic sauce, pita, rice and potatoes. "It's a promising smell, and so people want to know what it's about," says operations manager Marilyn Dib. "The response is that it's the best-tasting shawarma by far in the city. It maintains its juice."

Dib grew up in Ottawa and knows that the city's passion for shawarma dates back at least to her teen years. When her Lebanon-born husband Ibrahim (Brian) Mahmoud launched Cedars & Co. in 2009, naming it for Lebanon's most prominent tree, he wanted to bring shawarma to Old Ottawa South. The plan was to focus on Lebanese and other Mediterranean groceries, but Dib convinced him to broaden his scope. With the help of customer feedback, they now cater to special diets, including vegan, vegetarian, gluten-free, keto and halal. Lots of foods are local or Canadian, and there's a Mediterranean niche, but also plenty of Italian, East Indian and Mexican staples.

Beside the shawarma counter, which is also home to falafels, are two deli counters with prepared foods. One is filled with meat items, like samosas, kibbeh and beef-stuffed cabbage rolls. The other showcases vegan/vegetarian treats, like cabbage rolls, stuffed grape leaves, quinoa salad and Israeli couscous salad. It's no surprise to learn that Mahmoud owns five restaurants, including Lebanese Palace and Layal Shawarma and Bakery, and has a second branch of Cedars on Kilborn Avenue.

Address 1255 Bank Street, Ottawa, ON K1S 3Y2, +1 (613) 288-2797, www.facebook.com/
CedarsCo, brian@cedarsandco.ca | Getting there Bus 6 to Bank/Cameron | Hours Daily
8am–9pm | Tip Eat manakeesh (flatbreads) with za'atar and cheese at Fairouz Café, which
creates modern Middle Eastern fare (15 Clarence Street, www.fairouz.ca).

22 — Celtic Cross
Monument to workers who died building the canal

A mosquito is one of five unusual images engraved on a stone Celtic cross that rests at the foot of the Rideau Canal locks. The other images are an Irish harp, a pick and shovel, a wheelbarrow and an explosion. An inscription on the granite base states, *In memory of 1000 workers & their families who died building this canal 1826–1832.*

Workers at the time were building a canal with picks, shovels, chisels and mallets. Irish immigrants, French Canadians and First Nations people died from accidents, the cold weather, malaria, dysentery and smallpox while doing dangerous work in extreme conditions and with inadequate housing. Workers had no protection from the mosquitos that carried a temperate form of malaria. It seems strange to realize that malaria once killed people here in Canada, but the disease was rampant.

The original memorial cross was unveiled on June 27, 2004, by the Ottawa and District Labour Council. It's just off the paved foot/bike path in the trees south of the Fairmont Château Laurier. In August 2017, the cross was mysteriously knocked over and broken. A replacement was unveiled on April 29, 2018.

The Rideau Canal National Historic Site, managed by Parks Canada, links the Ottawa River to Lake Ontario through 202 kilometres (125 miles) of gravity-fed canals connected by channels, locks and dams. It was built under Lieutenant Colonel John By after the War of 1812, when the British Army needed a safe supply route that bypassed the St. Lawrence River and the United States border. The oldest continuously operating canal in North America, it's also a UNESCO World Heritage Site with 24 lock stations and 47 locks, if you include the tiny Tay Canal. UNESCO calls it "the best-preserved example of a slackwater canal in North America." The canal is also considered one of the greatest engineering feats of the 19th century.

Address Ottawa River Pathway/Trans-Canada Trail, Ottawa, ON K1A 0A4 | Getting there Bus 58 to Carling/Andrew Haydon Park | Hours Unrestricted | Tip The ByWard Market branch of Giant Tiger has an aging mural by Pierre Hardy hidden in its narrow alley/loading dock that's called *A Tribute to Franco-Ontarians* (98 George Street, www.gianttiger.com).

23 Champlain Oaks

Rallying around heritage trees

The leafy Champlain Park neighbourhood is home to dozens of bur oak trees that are upwards of 120–200 years old and have a quirky connection to French explorer Samuel de Champlain. Start your visit at the west side of the Champlain Park Fieldhouse, where you'll see a display case holding a cross-section of a tree that dates to 1856 and was felled by infill construction. Inside the fieldhouse there are interpretive panels.

The 2013 "Trees as Witnesses to History" display beside the cross-section celebrates the 400th anniversary of Champlain's trip up the Ottawa River and today's urban forest. For more than 10,000 years, the exhibit explains, a bur oak forest lined the Ottawa River between Chaudière Falls and Deschênes Rapids. The First Nations people ate the acorns, and European explorers recorded the trees (for use in shipbuilding) on maps and in journals.

Champlain travelled the river in 1613 and lost his astrolabe (a navigation device). In 1857, the tree from this cross-section on display grew in a forest near what's now Northwestern Avenue. Ten years later, someone found the astrolabe, and riverboat captain Daniel Keyworth Cowley acquired it. In 1903, Cowley's son R. H. Cowley subdivided land near his family's homestead to create Champlain Park. In 1945, builders left many bur oaks in place as the community expanded, and this tree grew around a chain in a fence. But in 2011, the tree, one of the last "forest-born bur oaks," was cut down for new development.

Forests Ontario recognized four "healthy, pre-settlement Bur Oak trees descended directly from the open forest of the Ottawa River shoreline" in 2017 under its Heritage Tree Program and later added three more. One, at 124 Cowley Avenue, is the area's second oldest heritage tree. It is 107 centimetres at chest height and about 180 years old. Visit other Champlain oaks along Daniel and Keyworth Avenues.

Address Champlain Park Field House, 149 Cowley Avenue, Ottawa, ON K1Y 0G6, www.champlainoaks.net | Getting there Bus 16 to Clearview/Carleton | Hours Unrestricted | Tip The Ottawa Mosque, home to the Ottawa Muslim Association, is the city's oldest and dates to 1964. It boasts a central dome and raised minaret (251 Northwestern Avenue, www.ottawamosque.ca).

24 Château Lafayette

The most colourful tavern in town

The Château Lafayette is old enough to lay claim to the title of "original Canadian dive bar." It opened in 1849 as Grant's Hotel, making it younger than the Rideau Canal (1832) but older than the city (1855) and Canada (1867). It has gone by many names: Exchange Hotel, Salmon's Hotel, Johnson House, Dominion House, Bodega Hotel. But after becoming the Château Lafayette in 1936 to be more welcoming to French-Canadians, it has simply been known as the Laff.

This old-school watering hotel offers live music and serves honest food – *poutine*, steamed hot dogs, smoked meat sandwiches and even Quebec's beloved deep-fried Jos Louis. And beer. Labatt 50 is stubbornly popular, and the 1849 Ale brewed for it by Big Rig Brewery honours its birth. Every Saturday around 4 pm, since November 3, 1999, country music sensation / entertainer Ron Burke takes the stage for his one-man Lucky Ron Show.

There's always someone to see here, be it Justin Bieber, Dan Aykroyd, an athlete or a politician. But in the older, more colourful days, the tavern almost certainly did time as a brothel, got itself haunted and earned the nickname "the bucket of blood." It has been Ottawa's oldest tavern ever since the Commercial Tavern burned down in 1982, and its red neon sign is likely the oldest in town. The Scott family has leased the building since 1966, steering the Laff through a rocky patch when the city banned smoking in restaurants and bars in 2001.

The first time the Laff appeared in the history books was as Grant's Hotel, when the Stony Monday Riot took place on York Street on September 17, 1849. Conservatives (Tories) and Reformists clashed over a bill to compensate everyone except those convicted of treason for property destroyed during a Lower Canada rebellion. People took shelter from the chaos in the fledgling hotel, and, as the Laff likes to say, still come seeking shelter.

Address 42 York Street, Ottawa, ON K1N 5S6, +1 (613) 241-4747, www.thelaff.ca, orders@thelaff.ca | **Getting there** O-Train to Rideau (Line 1) | **Hours** Daily 11–2am | **Tip** Union Local 613 is a rare Southern-style restaurant that serves grits and has a basement speakeasy hidden behind a bookcase (315 Somerset Street W, www.union613.ca).

25 Château Vanier

Ryan Reynolds once lived here

Canada celebrates its heroes, even when they decamp to the US, like Ryan Reynolds, the self-deprecating Hollywood heavyweight who starred in Marvel's *Deadpool* franchise and *The Proposal*, married actor Blake Lively, became a dad and won a 2021 Governor General's Performing Arts Award from Mary Simon. Much is made of the fact that Reynolds was born in Vancouver, but he also spent part of his childhood in Ottawa's Vanier neighbourhood.

At the start of the pandemic, Reynolds was lauded for charitable donations, including one to the Ottawa Food Bank. "Blake and I are so happy to give back to a country that has given us so much," he wrote in a message that was shared on the food bank's Instagram page in April 2020. "I happily have Canada running through my blood. So excited for the country to get through these tough times. I used to live in Ottawa (in Vanier). It holds a special place in my heart. So happy to donate to your amazing food bank."

"Where in Vanier? Need to put a plaque," tweeted one curious Ottawan. "I lived in a high rise. There were three in a row," Reynolds replied. "I thought they were called, 'The Vanier Towers.' I looked it up and they now seem to be business towers. My memory's a little foggy. I was around 13 yrs old at the time but I wasn't particularly bright for my age." When another user shared a photo of Château Vanier, Reynolds confirmed "That's it!"

Château Vanier is a condo complex completed in 1971 with three 17-storey towers known as A, B and C. The Quartier Vanier Business Improvement Association put the towers on a fundraising t-shirt as a tribute to Reynold's food bank donation and fond Vanier memories. And now the city is planning for a Ryan Reynolds Way, only it will be in a new east-end subdivision. "This is an incredible honour and a deal is a deal, Mr Mayor," tweeted Reynolds. "I've changed my daughter's name to 'Ottawa'."

Address 158 McArthur Avenue, Vanier, ON K1L 8E9 | Getting there Bus 14 to McArthur/Vanier | Hours Unrestricted | Tip Colombian arepas are on offer at Toasty Arepas, which opened during the pandemic and quickly earned a loyal fan base (51 Marier Avenue, www.toastyarepasottawa.ca).

26 — Chaudière Falls
The birthplace of Ottawa's electricity

The name doesn't begin to capture the story of this place. Chaudière Falls today is a 29-megawatt hydroelectric station that feeds into the provincial grid and powers 20,000 homes. Run by Portage Power, a subsidiary of Hydro Ottawa, it was off-limits for a century. Then, the historic site opened in 2017 as a public space with viewing platforms and information about the area's First Nations history and industrialist past. The complex, on Chaudière Island between Ontario and Quebec, is also home to Canada's oldest operating hydro station.

Algonquin Anishinaabe and other First Nations called the river Kichi Sibi, or the Great River. The original cauldron-shaped falls are a sacred site for the First Nations people as a meeting and offering place, portage site and trade route. The Algonquin First Nation named this spot Asticou, usually translated as "kettle" or "boiling water." French explorers called it Chaudière, or "kettle."

For early European explorers this area was a gateway to the country's interior. After the region was colonized and the river dammed, the falls were essential to the industrial boom of the mid-1800s by providing waterpower for the lumber mills and factories along the shoreline. Built between 1907 and 1909, the Ring Dam regulates water flow through the complex.

Designed by Indigenous architect Douglas Cardinal, the five-storey powerhouse that opened in 2017 is built below ground with green space and viewing platforms on the roof. "Every day, we work to be a leader in clean, green, sustainable power generation," says Portage Power on its website. "Chaudière Falls has six run-of-the-river hydroelectric facilities harnessing the natural flow of the river, while producing no waste and emitting no carbon dioxide." Downstream spawning beds help endangered sturgeon, and a bypass system and ladders protect endangered American eel migrating upstream.

Address Chaudière Island, Ottawa, ON, https://chaudierefalls.com, community@portagepower.com | Getting there Bus 61, 63, 66, 75, 85 to Booth/Chaudière | Hours Unrestricted | Tip An 1880 rail bridge called the Prince of Wales Bridge is now a multi-use, all-season pathway between Ottawa and Gatineau called the Chief William Commanda Bridge (eastern side of Lemieux Island, www.ottawa.ca).

27 Chemical Warfare Volunteers Plaque

Belated acknowledgement for a secret project

Chemical Warfare Defences and Counter-measures, reads the title of a plaque, which boasts five paragraphs of background information and is mounted on a stone block near a fence overlooking Rideau Falls and Green Island. It's a war-era story that Canada had to keep secret for years, and a suitably understated monument tucked in between the National Research Council's (NRC) parking lot and the NRC Central Heating and Cooling Plant.

Remembering the horrors of chemical warfare on the battlefields of the First World War, Canadians took up the task of researching and developing defences against chemical warfare in the 1930s, the plaque explains. Scientists at two key institutions, Ottawa's Chemical Warfare Laboratories and the Experimental Station in Suffield, Alberta, spearheaded the development of mechanisms to protect the Allied Forces against these toxic substances during World War II.

In August 1941, the federal government allowed the Chemical Warfare Laboratories (CWL) to set up at the former W. C. Edwards & Co. pulp and paper mill at Sussex Drive and John Street (now Rideau Falls Park and Canada's Centre for Geography and Exploration). Building on work by NRC staff, military test volunteers and National Defence scientists "advanced the protective capability of Canada's military through exceptional research and development that remains relevant even today."

Because the project was shrouded in secrecy, their contributions couldn't be publicly acknowledged. Finally, on April 24, 2005, people gathered for the plaque unveiling. Larry Capstick and Rob Collins, volunteer interpreters at the Canadian War Museum, have led public walks about military memorials and strive to include this one, but it does not get the attention it deserves.

Address 98 Sussex Drive, Ottawa, ON M5S 1K3, behind the N.R.C. Central Heating and Cooling Plant | Getting there Bus 9 to Sussex/King Edward | Hours Unrestricted | Tip *Remember Flanders* shows a bronze Lieutenant-Colonel John McCrae with a notebook with the words to *In Flanders Fields*, his poem that led to people remembering war dead with poppies (Green Island Park, www.canada.ca).

28 Chinatown's Royal Arch
A highly symbolic gateway

Chinatown wouldn't be Chinatown without an arch. Ottawa's arch, a special royal arch fit for a capital city, was unveiled on October 7, 2010, as a joint project with Beijing, Ottawa's Sister City. Several dozen artisans and technicians from China completed it in six months. The arch marked the 40th anniversary of diplomatic relations between the countries.

A symbol of prosperity, health and good fortune, this Beijing-designed royal arch is 12 metres (40 feet) high and has nine golden roofs covered with glazed tiles – only capital cities are entitled to have nine roofs. There are five symbolic coins of five precious metals (gold, silver, copper, iron and tin) embedded in the arch, as well as five threads (red, yellow, blue, white and black). *By following these Chinese traditions, it is said to bring blessings to the people and to the land*, reads a plaque.

The paifang-style arch looks like wood but is made of reinforced concrete and stone. Chinese characters on a centre blue panel say, "Ottawa Chinatown," and the intricate arch is rich in dragons and other symbols. Two mythical beasts, a mix of ferocious animals like lions and tigers, are found at the base of each red column. Half a kilogram of gold leaf was used on the vibrantly coloured arch. And two carved stone lions at street level are charged with guarding the gateway. They face east towards a 3D sculptural mural that shows a dragon running in front of the gateway as a police officer clocks its speed on radar – the police co-sponsored the work.

Until the First World War, this area drew working-class Irish and Italian immigrants. Then Chinese immigrants started opening businesses and were joined by a burst of Vietnamese newcomers in 1979 (see ch. 96). The area has 120 businesses today. Somerset Street Chinatown Business Improvement Area calls the area "a multicultural village with Asian flavour."

Address Somerset Street W (west of Bronson Avenue), Ottawa, ON K1R 6P3, www.ottawachinatown.ca, info@ottawachinatown.ca | **Getting there** O-Train to Pimisi (Line 1), then walk 13 minutes | **Hours** Unrestricted | **Tip** Shanghai restaurant has been in Chinatown since 1971 and is beloved for China Doll, its resident karaoke queen who performs Saturdays (651 Somerset Street W, www.theshang.wordpress.com).

29 __ Civic Pharmacy Sign
Spot the palindrome

The quietly memorable building has been a fixture at Carling and Holland since September 17, 1960, and a treasured example of mid-century modern commercial architecture. The former Civic Pharmacy building, now the Ukrainian Credit Union building, was created to "make this corner as comfortable as possible," according to a 1960 *Ottawa Citizen* article. It claimed to showcase Canada's first revolving, illuminated sign. The multi-coloured sign has long been lauded for its Googie style, a type of fun, modern, futurist architecture full of glass, steel and neon that was inspired by car culture, jets, the Space Age and the Atomic Age of the late 1940s to early 1970s.

The pharmacy sign originally rotated letter by letter because the five-letter word "civic" is a palindrome and reads the same forward and backward. But in 2017, after the anchor building went up for sale, area residents feared the sign might be scrapped. Luckily, the Ukrainian Credit Union saw the value of preserving it and restoring some of the building's original charms for its flagship Ottawa branch. "Literally in our first discussion we said, 'Wow look at this sign. It's got to have some historical value,'" remembers Slawko Borys, chair of the credit union's board of directors. "We also pride ourselves in being part of the broader community."

Ray Neon Signs updated the sign, decades after working on the original. The changes are subtle. The new sign lights up with LED lights instead of neon and can no longer rotate. New letter boxes – blue, yellow green, orange and red – now have white letters instead of black. And the credit union logo and name have replaced the "pharmacy" portion of the sign. So, although this treasured building has had different owners over the years and different logos and names attached to it, its famous sign continues to go by its historic nickname – the Civic Pharmacy sign.

Address 474–476 Holland Avenue, Ottawa, ON K1Y 4G6, +1 (613) 288-0206, www.ukrainiancu.com | Getting there Bus 53, 80, 86, 89 to Holland/Carling | Hours Unrestricted | Tip The Elgin Street Diner boasts a window full of five classic neon signs, with important messages like *Open 24 hours* and *Burgers shakes & fries* (374 Elgin Street, www.elginstreetdiner.com).

30 Colonnade Pizza
Annie Murphy vouches for this pie

Schitts Creek star Annie Murphy, of Alexis Rose fame, is possibly the biggest celebrity that Ottawa has ever produced, other than Alanis Morissette of course (see ch. 2). Whenever she's asked to name her favourite hometown hotspots, her answer is Colonnade Pizza. "If there is one piece of life-altering information I can share with you, it's this: whatever you do, no matter what, even if you're only in Ottawa for one tiny hour, GO TO COLONNADE PIZZA," she told *Hello!* magazine in 2018. "I've eaten an embarrassing amount of pizza in my lifetime, and this is. By far. My favourite. Pizza. In. The. Entire. World. There's no doubt in my mind that a pizza from Colonnade Pizza would be my last meal request."

In its own charming way, Colonnade Pizza has not capitalized on the recommendation or named a signature pizza after Annie. "Colonnade Pizza hasn't changed much in the 30+ years I've been in Ottawa," says Ottawa Tourism's Jantine Van Kregten, "and that's why people love it. It's definitely old school: delicious, greasy (in a good way!), cheesy pizza! I've only ever had pizza there ... I'm not even sure what else is on the menu." For the record, on top of the array of signature or DIY pizzas, there are pastas, salads, chicken brochettes, wings, *poutine* and sides. But everyone's here for the pizza.

The family-run pizzeria launched in 1967 with the Metcalfe Street branch and has grown to include four more franchises in Ottawa South's Blue Heron Mall, Merivale, Barrhaven and the west end. Kalil Dahdouh took over the pizzeria on November 4, 1967, after moving here from Lebanon, working his way up in the restaurant business and taking over an existing restaurant space. The secret to Colonnade's success is apparently the homemade tomato sauce and its secret recipe, along with a custom brick cheese from the Oak Grove Cheese Factory in New Hamburg, five hours away.

Address 1500 Bank Street, Ottawa, ON K1H 7Z2, +1 (613) 737-1107, www.colonnadepizza.com | Getting there Bus 6 to Bank/Karn | Hours Daily 11am–9pm | Tip Drag dinners, vegan and gluten-free afternoon tea, and children's afternoon tea in an opulent space are on tap at the Vanitea Room (551 Somerset Street W, www.thevanitearoomteasalon.com).

31 Commissioners Park Tulips

A princess is born, a nation sends perennial thanks

Ottawa's connection to tulips dates back to January 19, 1943, when Princess Margriet of the Netherlands was born to Queen Juliana and Prince Bernhard at Ottawa Civic Hospital. The Dutch royals took refuge here during World War II to escape the occupation of the Netherlands by Nazi Germany. So, the Canadian government temporarily declared the hospital's maternity ward "extraterritorial," turning it into "international territory," and the royal baby became Dutch and not Dutch-Canadian.

Then, in 1945, Canadian troops helped liberate the Netherlands, and the Dutch government sent 100,000 tulip bulbs to Ottawa in thanks. The gesture continues each fall, and the Canadian Tulip Festival takes place every May.

The National Capital Commission calls itself "the official gardener of Canada's capital" and plants nearly one million tulips every year in 120 flower beds at 30 locations. Commissioners Park has 30 of the planting beds and more than 100 varieties of tulips that include early-, middle- and late-season blooms. Notably, it's home to the Queen Juliana Gift Bed with bulbs gifted by the Netherlands. The festival designates it as Bed 1 and it is closest to Dows Lake Pavilion. Also look for Bed 16, where landscape architects test new varieties before mass planting them in regular flower beds.

Commissioners Park showcases a staggering 250,000 tulips each spring. Tulips come in every shade except blue (any with the word "blue" in their names are technically shades of violet), and everyone has their favourites. Admire everything from Happy People (cream and yellow) and Royal Virgin (pure white) to Fabio (deep red with a yellow fringe) and Weber's Parrot (cream, green and pink tulip with oversized, crinkled petals). Some lucky tulips get chosen to live another year, but others are donated to non-profits and schools or composted for use in gardens across the region.

Address Preston Street and Queen Elizabeth Driveway, Ottawa, ON K1S 4N7, +1 (613) 239-5000, www.ncc-ccn.gc.ca, info@ncc-ccn.ca | Getting there Bus 85 to Preston/Carling | Hours Unrestricted, tulips bloom in May | Tip The Dows Lake Pavilion rents skates, snowshoes and sleighs in winter, and canoes, kayaks, bikes, stand-up paddleboards and paddleboats in summer (1001 Queen Elizabeth Driveway, www.dowslake.com).

32 Confederation Park Fountain

Evidence of war and a possible haunting

Take a good look at the fountain in Confederation Park to find intriguing shrapnel nicks on the basin rim that reportedly speak to a more dangerous time in another country. From roughly 1843 to 1948, two virtually identical red granite fountains, designed by Sir Charles Barry, architect of the British Houses of Parliament, stood together in London's Trafalgar Square. They endured the bombings of World War II at the hands of Nazi Germany during the Blitz, which lasted eight months in 1940 and 1941. The modest fountains miraculously survived relatively unscathed, but they were eventually replaced by larger, grander fountains. In 1955, the fountains were given to Canada and separated, one finding a new home in Ottawa and the other in Wascana Centre on the grounds of the Saskatchewan Legislative Buildings in Regina.

Ottawa's fountain was dedicated on October 5, 1955, to the memory of Lieutenant Colonel John By on an embankment leading to the Laurier Bridge. By founded Bytown, which was later renamed Ottawa, and famously supervised construction of the Rideau Canal (see ch. 22). The fountain was later rebuilt, and on May 25, 1975, it was relocated to Confederation Park and re-dedicated. Throughout 2019 and 2020, it was fenced and underwent significant repairs.

The Haunted Walk of Ottawa tour guides have been telling the fountain's story for 25 years. "The fountain is kind of both a secret and a mystery hiding in plain sight," says Jim Dean, creative director of Haunted Walks Inc. Legend has it that the body of a murdered man was found floating in one of the fountains (no one knows which) in England and that a ghostly corpse may be lurking. One of the company's tour guides has had two experiences – first as a child, then as an adult – chatting with a man sitting on the edge of the fountain who likely was not really there.

Address Corner of Elgin Street and Laurier Avenue, Ottawa ON K1P 5J2, +1 (613) 239-5000, https://ncc-ccn.gc.ca/places/confederation-park | Getting there O-Train to Parliament (Line 1) | Hours Unrestricted | Tip The York Street Millennium Fountain (corner of York Street and Sussex Drive) commemorates an era when water wasn't "freely available to all" and people had to buy it from water carriers or fetch it from public wells.

33__ *Corso Italia* Mural
Postcard-style memories of the past

The logical gateway to Little Italy is Preston and Gladstone, where the 2013 *Bambini* sculpture stands, technically representing a child's drawing of a soccer team but widely nicknamed "the bowling pins." But it actually makes more sense to begin a visit here in the middle of the neighbourhood, taking stock of the past. Find your way under the Trans-Canada Highway (Highway 417 or the Queensway) to the *Corso Italia Heritage* Mural that covers the concrete walls on both sides of the underpass. The 30-plus murals are postcard-style panels commissioned by families, businesses and groups and painted by Ottawa-born artist Karole Marois.

On the west wall, a background mural places you on Preston Street between Dow's Lake and the Ottawa River, and it boasts an old train and a nod to the logging industry. The east wall background mural speaks to the Italians who immigrated to Canada via Pier 21 in Halifax between 1945 and 1965 with a white ship and silhouettes of newly arrived immigrants. The murals, Marois writes on a 2004 plaque, *have been designed to represent the windows of the ship offering a glimpse into important contributors and events in the evolution of Italian heritage in Ottawa.*

The mural project was spearheaded by Joe Cotroneo, who owns Pub Italia and the Vintage Italian Moto Museum (see ch. 105). The mural for Preston Hardware, established in 1945, honours its place as "Ottawa's first self-serve hardware." The Trattoria Caffé Italia mural shows people sharing food in a warm, colourful space. The Prescott, which dates to 1934 as the Preston Hotel, features a vintage car. Another mural honours St. Anthony's Day, which starts with an outdoor mass on the steps of St. Anthony's Church and ends with a feast. In the centre of the underpass, a street sign points the way to 14 current businesses, like Simply Biscotti, Frank's Auto Centre and Pasticceria Gelateria.

Address Preston Street underpass of the Trans-Canada Highway / Queensway, Ottawa, ON K1R 7R6 | **Getting there** Bus 85 to Preston / Young | **Hours** Unrestricted | **Tip** Par-Tee Putt is Ottawa's only mini-putt bar, and it's in a subterranean space in Little Italy. The 18 mini-putt holes showcase iconic landmarks (379 Preston Street, www.parteeputt.com / ottawa).

34 Cottage Gas Station
Ode to the days of full service

Back in the early years of private car ownership, motorists bought gas in cans from hardware stores, general stores and blacksmith shops. The US got its first full-service gas station in Pittsburgh in 1913. Here, at Richmond Road and Island Park Drive, a service station first owned by Benzolene Corporation opened June 30, 1934, along what was then the main highway into Ottawa from the rural West.

This rare example of a pre-World War II service station – small, irregularly shaped and clad in pale yellow stucco – was granted heritage status in 2015, although it's currently vacant and fenced. It was built in the Tudor Revival style to blend in with neighbouring houses. This English cottage boasts a rounded-arch doorway, round-headed windows, rectangular windows with overhanging shed roofs, twin chimneys and a steeply pitched gable roof. There's a house-style commercial section, adjoining office area and two-bay service station. In granting Ontario Heritage Act status, the city's Built Heritage Sub-committee lauded the station's architecture, location and historical value.

Jeff Leiper, councillor for the Kitchissippi Ward, and others call the heritage building "the old cottage gas station." Artist, author and history buff Andrew King celebrated the "architectural rarity" in a 2014 *Ottawa Citizen* article. Purchased for $1 in 1937 by Champlain Oil Products, it's also known as the former Champlain Oil Service Station. Charles-Émile Trudeau, father and grandfather to Canadian prime ministers, owned Champlain and made his fortune in Montreal gas stations.

The building spent time as a used car dealership. A developer floated the idea of turning it into a coffeehouse with a drive thru. At the moment, the Trinity Group hopes to relocate it to the front of the property and wrap a mixed-use building around it, as heritage status only protects the outside and location.

Address 70 Richmond Road, Ottawa, ON M5C 1N8 | Getting there Bus 11, 51 (direction Britannia) to Richmond/Island Park | Hours Unrestricted | Tip Danny Hussey's Central Art Garage is a contemporary art gallery and art framing studio in a reclaimed auto mechanic garage in Chinatown (66B Lebreton Street N, www.centralartgarage.com).

35 Cundell Stables

Downtown's hidden horse stable

Since 1890, the name Cundell has been synonymous with horses in downtown Ottawa. John Cundell is still allowed to keep a stable in his ByWard Market yard and take people for rides in a romantic carriage for four or a larger, well-padded wagon over to Parliament Hill or Rideau Hall. His grandfather and father were both involved in the family business, using horses to help with construction, aid the fire department, and handle bread and dairy deliveries. Then it was on to city garbage and snow-plowing contracts and supplying ponies for birthday parties and summer cottagers.

John has lived in the same house his whole life. He drove his first horse team when he was 12 and used to break in and then show ponies. He has three Belgian draft horses (Jake, Flash and Robbie) and three miniature ponies (Queen, Jill and Janelle), although his stables could hold up to 17. He remembers when everybody had horses in their backyards.

"We're the last one for the last 50 years or maybe longer. Now the city is getting so big and where we live, it's so busy. The bus drivers go fast right by you." His dad drove the likes of Paul Anka, Gene Autry and John Diefenbaker. John once took Prime Minister Pierre Trudeau for a spin.

Cundell Stables offers year-round rides that meander through the market and towards Rideau Hall. Be prepared to wave to enchanted passersby on an hour-long jaunt. To book, call John since he doesn't have a website, email or social media. The ByWard Market BIA hires him to give short rides on holidays and special occasions. "You meet a lot of nice people," says John. "I love driving the horses. When I'm out doing that, I'm in heaven. You deal with only happy people that get on my wagon. But it's getting harder all the time." If there aren't enough rides booked, he and his wife Patty hitch up the horses and exercise them at least three times a week.

Address 113 York Street, Ottawa, ON K1N 5T4, +1 (613) 241-8054 | **Getting there** O-Train to Rideau (Line 1) | **Hours** By appointment | **Tip** First Bite Treats brings "croffles" – waffles made from croissant dough – to the city. Try the one with crushed Lotus Biscoff cookies (531A Sussex Drive, www.firstbitetreats.ca).

36 Delegation of the Ismaili Imamat

Doing the Aga Khan's work

Designed by Tokyo-based architect Fumihiko Maki, the Delegation of the Ismaili Imamat is the award-winning home to the Aga Khan Foundation Canada and gives a permanent diplomatic representation for the Aga Khan Development Network (AKDN). "The building is really our mission to Canada, and it serves essentially a number of functions," says Dr. Mahmoud Eboo, the delegation's representative. "One is it operates as an embassy. Second is it operates as a space for engagement." It was inaugurated December 6, 2008, by His Highness the Aga Khan, the 49th hereditary Imam, or spiritual leader, of the Shia Imami Ismaili Muslims and founder and chairman of the AKDN.

The three-storey building, neighbour to the Saudi Arabian and Korean embassies, was inspired by a rock crystal and stands for openness and transparency. "The idea is to inspire open thinking, dialogue and the ability to look at different perspectives and to respect different perspectives," explains Eboo. The atrium, with its asymmetrical glass roof structure, has views of all corners of the property. The atrium's *jali* (Hindi for net) screen is reinterpreted from a traditional perforated stone or carved wood screen in modern sand-cast aluminum, with a double layer of repeating hexagons.

The building is mainly clad in Neopariés, crystallized glass panels that create a smooth, opaque surface. An interior courtyard provides a modern interpretation of a *charbagh*, or four-part garden of historic Islamic landscape architecture in South and Central Asia. The same architect later designed the Aga Khan Museum in Toronto.

The Delegation has hosted conferences, exhibitions, roundtables, book launches and interactive workshops that promote learning and dialogue on international development and humanitarian issues.

Address 199 Sussex Drive, Ottawa, ON K1N 1K6, +1 (613) 237-2532, www.akfc.ca, akfc.info@akdn.org | Getting there Bus 9 to Boteler/Dalhousie | Hours Unrestricted from outside, tours by appointment | Tip 1 Elgin restaurant at the National Arts Centre, has a canal-side patio with a retractable glass roof and sides that extends patio season (1 Elgin Street, www.nac-cna.ca/en/1elgin).

37 Diefenbunker
The ultimate Cold War relic

Just 30 minutes from Parliament Hill in rural Ottawa lies a former Cold War bunker that is now a not-for-profit museum/escape room. The Diefenbunker: Canada's Cold War Museum is a four-storey, underground bunker built between 1959 and 1961 to shelter key federal government and military officials during the Cold War in the event of a nuclear war. It was officially known as Central Emergency Government Headquarters (CEGHQ Carp) and was the largest of a series of bunkers built across Canada during tensions between the United States and the former Soviet Union and their allies. It was irreverently dubbed "the Diefenbunker" after Prime Minister John Diefenbaker.

The fortified bunker boasts 100,000 square feet over four levels. Made of 32,000 cubic yards of hand-poured concrete and 5,000 tons of steel, it was secretly built on a former farm just below the peak of a natural ridge to withstand a five-megaton nuclear blast from 1.8 kilometres away. Only a small portion of it was visible on the surface – the rest goes up to 75 feet underground.

The Diefenbunker was almost used during the Cuban Missile Crisis but never served its intended purpose. It operated from 1961 to 1994 as the hub of a communications network and civil defence system and as Canadian Forces Station (CFS) Carp, with a staff of up to 150 people on 24-hour shift rotations. The cupboards and pantries were permanently stocked with enough food and rations to feed 535 people for 30 days.

The Diefenbunker got National Historic Site status in 1994, and CFS Carp was closed the same year. The decommissioned building languished until becoming a not-for-profit museum in 1997. Guided tours cover all four levels, including the blast tunnel, medical centre, war cabinet room and Bank of Canada vault. Sign up for bunker birthdays, spy camps and the Escape Manor, which bills itself as the world's largest escape room.

Address 3929 Carp Road, Carp, ON K0A 1L0, +1 (613) 839-0007, www.diefenbunker.ca, reservations@diefenbunker.ca | Getting there By car, take Highway 417 to the Carp Road Exit, number 166, turn north onto Carp Road, drive 8 to 10 minutes, and look for the Diefenbunker sign on the west side of the road | Hours Wed–Fri 10am–4pm, Sat & Sun 10am–3pm | Tip The Carp Fair dates to 1863 and runs every September, but it also runs drive-in bingos (with pie) as a fundraiser in the summer (Carp Fairgrounds, 3790 Carp Road, Carp, www.carpfair.ca).

38 École Guigues

Franco-Ontarian landmark

A heritage condo and community centre in a former school is considered a symbol for Francophone rights in Ontario. It tells the story of the battle against Regulation 17, a 1912 Ontario Government law that effectively outlawed French-language education in primary schools by capping French classes to one hour a day and banning primary schools from using French as a language of instruction or communication beyond Grade 2. The government then created Regulation 18 to revoke certification from teachers and funding from schools that disobeyed.

In January 1916, École Guigues parents, many armed with hatpins and other household items, occupied the lobby and front steps to protect teachers. The successful battle with police sparked other protests and ultimately forced the government to stop enforcing Regulation 17 in 1927 and repeal it in 1944. The hatpin, a long decorative pin used to hold hats to heads, became a symbol for French-language rights in Ontario. In 2016, Canada's then Prime Minister Kathleen Wynne apologized for Regulation 17 and commended Franco-Ontarians for "tremendous courage and tenacity" in the long struggle to protect Francophone culture.

Heritage Ottawa says the 1904 Guigues School was named for Ottawa's first Roman Catholic bishop and designed by Ottawa architect Félix Maral Hamel in the Neo-Classical style. It expanded in 1923–1924 but closed in 1979 because of declining enrolment and rising maintenance costs. It earned heritage status in 1980 and did a stint as an emergency shelter. In 1994, it was sold to the Centre polyvalent des aînés francophones d'Ottawa-Carleton who made a seniors community centre on the lower two floors and 14 condos designed by architect Barry Padolsky on the upper two floors. The Centre de services Guigues opened on May 30, 1997, and won the city's Architectural Conservation Award of Excellence for Adaptive Reuse.

Address 159 Murray Street, Ottawa, ON K1N 5M7, www.heritageottawa.ca | Getting there O-Train to Rideau (Line 1), then walk 10 minutes | Hours Unrestricted | Tip Rockcliffe Park has a secret swimming hole called The Pond that used to be a gravel and sand quarry. Part of the Caldwell-Carver Conservation Area, it allows swimming from 7am to 2pm (Pond Street, www.rockcliffepark.ca).

39 Elizabeth Hay's Bookmark
Project Bookmark Canada celebrates CanLit

Project Bookmark Canada believes it's the world's only national, site-specific literary exhibit. Since 2009, the organization has been creating the "Canada's literary trail" by putting "Bookmarks," or pieces of stories and poems in the exact physical locations of imagined literary scenes. Each Bookmark is a poster-sized plaque with a passage of up to 500 words from a story or poem that people can read while standing in the footsteps of a character or narrator. There's also a blurb about the author and the registered charity.

Ottawa is home to Bookmark #5. It commemorates *Garbo Laughs*, a best-selling 2003 novel by Elizabeth Hay about writer Harriet Browning, who is "caught in a tug of war between real life and the films of the past" and forms a Friday-night movie club with friends and neighbours. Harriet is new to the city and lives in Old Ottawa South around the time of the massive 1998 North American ice storm.

Born in Owen Sound and writing since she was a teenager, Hay settled in Ottawa in 1992. *Garbo Laughs* was her second novel, and she has won multiple awards for her fiction and non-fiction, including the Scotiabank Giller Prize for *Late Nights On Air*. Unveiled on October 26, 2010, with Hay reading a scene from her book, the Bookmark is on a patch of green space in Old Ottawa South near the Rideau Canal.

The plaque is in Hay's neighbourhood, so she sees it often and is "touched and gratified every time." Sometimes fans find it and write to her. "They were hurrying past and paused, startled into another dimension," says Hay. "Suddenly they see where they are in a new light, as a real place under their feet that inspired a fictional book. It's as if they were in two places at once, each place more alive than it was before. For a moment the plaque turns Ottawa into an illustrated book, so to speak, and turns a novel into a piece of public art."

Address West side of Canal Woods Terrace at Fulton Avenue just south of Colonel By Drive, Ottawa, ON, +1 (905) 634-7516, www.projectbookmarkcanada.ca, info@projectbookmarkcanada.ca | Getting there Bus 10 to Bronson / Colonel By | Hours Unrestricted | Tip Owned by an Anishinaabe mother-daughter duo from Ondarez Clothing and Goods and Jayde Micah Designs, Beandigen Café is a hub for Indigenous business and culture (106 Exhibition Way, Unit 900).

40 Fairmont Château Laurier

A luxury hotel's tragic Titanic *ties*

On a wood pedestal in the lobby of the Fairmont Château Laurier is a white marble bust of Sir Wilfred Laurier that serves as a sombre reminder of the hotel's connection to the *Titanic*. The luxury hotel bears the name of the man who was prime minister in 1911 when it was being built. A lavish grand opening was slated for April 26, 1912, and both Laurier and Charles Melville Hays, hotel visionary and general manager of the Grand Trunk Railway, were planning to attend. Hays travelled to London to buy furniture for the dining room and was given a last-minute chance to sail on *Titanic*'s maiden voyage with his furniture in the cargo hold.

Around 11:40pm on April 14, 1912, the *Titanic* hit an iceberg near Newfoundland and quickly sank the next morning in the Atlantic Ocean, taking more than 1,500 passengers and crew with it. Hays perished. The furniture destined for Ottawa was also lost, and the Château Laurier delayed its grand opening to June 12 with an appropriately more modest affair.

As for the Laurier bust, Hays had commissioned Belgian-born, French-based sculptor Paul Chevré to create it for the railway hotel lobby. Chevré was also on the *Titanic* heading to Ottawa for the grand opening but jumped in a lifeboat and was one of the 700-plus survivors. He had sent the Laurier bust ahead on another ship, and so it arrived safely. Look for a photo of Hays – and the *Titanic* – in a lobby level hallway dedicated to archival photos.

The hotel known as "Ottawa's Castle" has since hosted countless famous guests and several famous residents. Pierre Elliot Trudeau lived here in the 1960s just before becoming prime minister and famously loved diving into the Art Deco pool. Renowned portrait photographer Yousef Karsh lived here for 18 years and had a studio on the sixth floor. Look for some of his photos in the Reading Lounge and more in the suite that bears his name.

Address 1 Rideau Street, Ottawa, ON K1N 8S7, +1 (613) 241-1414, www.fairmont.com/laurier-ottawa, chateaulaurier@fairmont.com | **Getting there** O-Train to Rideau (Line 1) | **Hours** Unrestricted | **Tip** Sleep in one of three vintage Airstream trailers – *Roy*, *Tom* and *Chelsea* – parked at KIN Vineyards. Vintage Hideaway runs seasonally (222 Craig's Side Road, Carp, www.vintagehideaway.ca).

41 Feline Café

Where cats and coffee co-exist

The one constant at the Feline Café since it opened in 2016 is that it's a place where cats needing forever homes can meet people seeking furry family members. Owner Josée Cyr launched by partnering with rescues and offering the café as a fostering location. They helped save more than 500 cats. In 2020, the café became the Feline Café Foundation and began doing its own rescues. What was once a lounge open to anybody evolved into a shop with a separate cat lounge to survive COVID. The lounge is by reservation only, and visitors must be at least 12 years old. Each 45-minute time slot comes with one drink. "We just love cats and we love coffee," says rescue manager Katherine Clements. "We're just so happy to be saving so many kitties."

When the foundation accepts a cat, it goes to a foster home to get ready for adoption. This involves vet visits, including shots and surgeries if needed, and socialization. "A lot of cats that we're saving have been living outside, and they're terrified," explains Clements. The café can hold seven to ten cats at a time, and they must like the company of other cats and enjoy the experience. Most animals stay at least a month, since change is disruptive. Matching the right cat to the right family is another jigsaw puzzle. Adoption fees typically range from $150 to $300, even when the foundation has poured thousands into vet bills for a kitten. "We're not in it for the money – that's for sure," says Clements. "We're in it for the kitties."

On the retail side is a mini grocery and gift shop with an espresso machine. Food is plant-based, so staff joke that "everything's vegan" here except the carnivorous cats. There are cat-themed masks, socks, pinch bowls, mugs, stirring spoons and lapel pins that make great gifts for cat-lovers, including yourself. For cats, there are catnip toys and cat grass kits. Human food includes vegan marshmallows and ketchup chips from Covered Bridge.

Address 1076 Wellington Street W, Ottawa, ON K1Y 2Y3, +1 (613) 680-6369, www.felinecafeottawa.com | Getting there Bus 11 to Wellington/Melrose | Hours Wed–Sun 11am–8pm | Tip Wabi Sabi is a community knitting hub that sells all the fixings to knit, crochet, felt, spin and weave and offers online and in-person classes (1078 Wellington Street W, www.wabi-sabi.ca).

42   Fish Sewer Grates

Civic infrastructure that conveys a message

Have you ever wondered why so many Ottawa sewer grates have fish on them? "Storm sewer grates are often marked with a fish symbol as a reminder that they drain into local rivers and streams," explains the city's website. "The fish symbol is there to remind the public that what goes down the drain can harm our rivers and streams. Remember: Only rain goes down the drain." That means put your cigarette butts, garbage and animal waste where they belong.

People who find and celebrate manhole covers are known as drain-spotters. In Japan, elaborate covers are works of art that tell local and regional stories, and there are even collectable cards. Calgary has an innovative public art program for manhole covers. But most cities make do with utilitarian covers featuring geometric patterns and perhaps their names and/or the names of the utility.

Ottawa has three types of sewers. Storm sewers carry rainfall and runoff to a stormwater pond or creek, stream or river. Sanitary sewers move wastewater from homes and businesses to the Robert O. Pickard Environmental Centre for treatment. Combined sewers in the downtown core carry wastewater and runoff to the treatment plant and can overflow. Drainage is an important issue for those who care about their local watershed.

Scout for fish sewer grates, and you'll fall in love with the nuances. Some are solid, raised designs, and some have openings in the fish "gills." They might be new, weathered or delightfully rusted. Some are on the road or sidewalk, and others wrap around a sidewalk edge with a gaping hole to the underground. On the non-fish front, Ottawa hydro has one with classic geometric shapes. Rarer ones say "Traffic/Circulation" and "Streetlighting Canada." Drain-spotter Kate Robertson even found a fun one at Rideau Terrace and Ridgeway Avenue that says "Ottawa" and "DANGER" – and features a toilet.

Address Northeast corner of Bank Street and Belmont Avenue, Ottawa, ON K1S 3X8 | Getting there Bus 6, 7 to Belmont/Bank | Hours Unrestricted | Tip The Downtown Rideau Business Improvement Area partnered with the city for a mural box program that wraps electrical boxes with works from local artists (various locations, www.downtownrideau.com).

43 Garlic King
Ottawa's most eccentric restaurateur

"I am the Garlic King / I can do anything," the Garlic King gleefully shouts to launch a 40-second song clip, "My Shawarma" that riffs off 1979's "My Sharona" by The Knack. "Give me some garlic with / some secret sauce / and I want some onions on / my shawarma / Ooh I can't believe the size / of those king fries / you gotta see the Garlic King / to get my shawarma," the song continues.

Adel Azzi, the Garlic King himself, struts around his Garlic King restaurant in a king's outfit, usually royal purple with gold trim, and waves from a snow globe-like dome jutting out of his souped-up Dodge Caravan. "Just Dave," his loyal sidekick with no title or last name, says the Lebanon-born Garlic King cooked his way up through the army and for the Lebanese prime minister and president before moving to Ottawa and opening Really Lebanese Food, Home of the Garlic King. Now simply the Garlic King, it's been an Ottawa institution for those in the know for nearly three decades.

"Anyone can make money. Not everyone can make friends," is the restaurant's slogan. Loyal customers come several times a week to feast on fattoush, tabouleh, falafels and other staples of the Mediterranean diet. They often order the family platter, which feeds four people with a pound of meat, drinks, sides and dessert for $50. The Garlic King has hobnobbed with politicians and celebrities, Just Dave says, but dubs former Governor General Michaëlle Jean "the coolest because she's the only one who actually let him come to Rideau Hall in his king outfit."

As for the van, it's custom wrapped with ads and logos and sports a gold crown and clear dome (made from shatterproof plastic) on the roof. It's most impressive at night when it's lit up, or during Santa's Parade of Lights every December in Orléans. "I work from my heart," the Garlic King says in an interview. "I like people to eat healthy food."

Address 2586 St. Joseph Boulevard, Orleans, ON K1C 1G3, +1 (613) 830-5464, www.thegarlicking.ca, info@thegarlicking.ca | **Getting there** Bus 31, 32 to St. Joseph/St. Jean | **Hours** Mon–Wed, Sat 11am–8:30pm, Thu & Fri 11am–9pm | **Tip** The Cumberland Heritage Village Museum showcases rural life in the 1920s and 1930s with a series of reconstructed village buildings, like a general store, one-room schoolhouse and garage (2490 Old Montreal Road, Cumberland, www.ottawa.ca).

44　Gatineau's Culture Trail
Ode to a legendary lumberjack

French Canadian folk hero Joseph "Jos" Montferrand was a larger-than-life character, so it's fitting that the lumberjack / strongman who worked the Ottawa River in the 1800s be honoured with an oversized sculpture on Gatineau's Culture Trail. Find him on a patch of grass at the otherwise unremarkable intersection of Rue Montcalm and Rue Hanson / Highway 50. *Whether as man or legend, Jos Montferrand has joined the great family of giants*, reads a bilingual interpretation sign about the giant and national hero.

Dis–moi, Ti-Jos, comment t'es devenu un géant (Tell me, Ti-Jos, how you became a giant) by artist Jean-Yves Vigneau shows Montferrand sitting on a stump contemplating a clear-cut forest. *At one time, not that long ago, the value of a man was measured by the number of trees he could fell between sunrise and sunset*, the sign explains. *Nowadays, the value of a man might be measured by the number of trees he planted.*"

The black wire frame was the basis of a 2017 portrayal of Montferrand as a "vegetal sculpture" at Mosaïcultures in Jacques-Cartier Park. It was then donated to the city by Mosaïcultures Internationales. Stompin' Tom Connors immortalized the six-foot-four legend, and some of the tall tales linked to him, in a song called "Big Joe Mufferaw."

Gatineau, population 285,000, is on the north shore of the Ottawa River, across from downtown Ottawa. Inspired by Boston's Freedom Trail, the Culture Trail is a three-kilometre stroll to see art, entertainment and points of interest. In summer, there are public readings and exhibitions. There are more than two dozen permanent stops, including a poetry trail with extracts from 30 poems attached to plaques on building façades. In summer, free one-hour guided tours leave from Promenade du Portage and Rue Laval twice a week. Pick up your trail map at Gatineau's Maison du Tourisme (103 Laurier Street).

Address Corner of Rue Montcalm and Rue Hanson, Gatineau, QC J8Y 3B5, www.gatineau.ca | Getting there Bus 20, 35, 48 to Montcalm / Hanson | Hours Unrestricted | Tip SOIF Bar à Vin is the creation of Véronique Rivest, the first woman to win at the World's Best Sommelier Competition when she took second place in 2013 (88 Rue Montcalm, Gatineau, www.soifbaravin.ca).

45 Gay Sweater

Using human hair to make a point

A sweater knit from human hair donated from lesbian, gay, bisexual, transgender and queer, intersex and asexual (LGBTQIA+) community members is one of the fascinating artifacts you'll find in the Canadian Museum of History. The *Gay Sweater* is a cardigan with rainbow buttons created by staff and volunteer spinners and knitters at the Canadian Centre for Gender and Sexual Diversity (CCGSD) to start conversations about sexual identity, bullying and belonging. The centre calls this "the world's first and only gay object."

According to the centre, "That's so gay," is one of the most common examples of bullying language, and that words like "gay" should not be used to describe anything negative. "I would love to grow up in a world where, 'That's so gay,' wasn't a thing," Jeremy Dias said in a 2015 YouTube video about the sweater, when it was unveiled and he was the centre's director. "In literalizing a gay sweater, I'm hoping that people will reflect on what they say and how they treat people."

The sweater is in the museum's Canadian History Hall, in the Modern Canada gallery that details 1914 to the present. More than 100 LGBTQIA+ adults donated hair in a multitude of shades for the sweater that weighs 1.8 kilograms and sports the label, "100% Gay." The sweater has been featured in more than 1,000 anti-bullying and anti-discrimination programs across Canada. "It really tells a multi-layered story," says James Trépanier, curator of Post-Confederation Canada.

The exhibits around the *Gay Sweater* detail how LGBTQIA+ Canadians were once widely perceived as deviant and faced social discrimination and even criminal charges. The federal government fired hundreds of LGBTQIA+ public servants in the 1960s as a perceived risk to national security. Later that decade, though, Bill C-150 decriminalized homosexual acts between two consenting adults in private. Canada legalized same-sex marriage in 2005.

ON Y PARLE
LE BULLYING
L'HOMOPHOBIE
LA TRANSPHOBIE
LA JOURNÉE
ROSE
LE 13 AVRIL 2016

IT'S TIME
TO TALK ABOUT
BULLYING
HOMOPHOBIA
TRANSPHOBIA
DAY OF PINK
APRIL 13, 2016

« Je ne veux pas être seulement quelqu'un qui porte un costume, être moi. »

Address 100 Laurier Street, Gatineau, QC K1A 0M8, +1 (819) 776-7000, www.historymuseum.ca | Getting there Bus 15 to Laurier/Élisabeth-Bruyère | Hours Wed, Fri–Sun 9am–5pm, Thu 9am–7pm | Tip Venus Envy Ottawa believes sex "should be dirty in a good way, not a shameful one," and so the education-oriented sex shop and bookstore sells "cool and sexy stuff" (226 Bank Street, www.venusenvy.ca).

46 Golden Palace

A secret recipe for open-ended eggrolls

The city's oldest Chinese restaurant dates back to April 12, 1960. This family-run chop suey house boasts a gloriously retro sign, a pagoda-style roof and an ornate dining room with gold and green handcrafted wooden ceiling squares that were shipped by boat from China and are hand-washed once a year. Enjoy the chop suey, fried rice and chicken balls, but come for the Famous Golden Palace Egg Rolls.

Six dedicated women arrive daily around 4am to spend about six hours assembling hundreds of egg rolls, which are tightly packed by hand with pork, cabbage, celery, onions and bean sprouts. The exact recipe is, naturally, a secret. The women use egg yolk to seal the edges of the egg roll wrappers, and they don't pinch the ends closed. Once fried in lard, the rolls come out crunchy and with "burnt ends." They are served with homemade plum sauce made with a little pumpkin purée for sweetness.

Bill Kwong, Golden Palace's third-generation owner, says, "Really we were the first restaurant that has this open-ended egg roll in Ottawa, but obviously copycats are all around." The creation story about whether this design is deliberate or a happy accident is murky. "To be honest with you," says Kwong, "when I was working here in high school it was already like that." Seven pages of customer testimonials are posted on the restaurant's website, with people like Andre in Timmins asking for "World's Greatest Egg Roll" t-shirts, and Evelyn in St. Catharines declaring, "You remain the Egg Roll Kings of Canada!"

Golden Palace sells egg rolls at the Canadian Tire Centre, home of the Ottawa Senators, and ships them frozen across Ontario. To celebrate its April 12 anniversary, it usually draws lineups for half-priced eggrolls. "I'm just grateful my family was able to develop something like this and that people just love it," says Kwong. "I just feel honoured to continue on this legacy."

Address 2195 Carling Avenue, Ottawa, ON K2B 7E8, +1 (613) 820-8444, www.goldenpalacerestaurant.ca | Getting there Bus 51, 85 to Carling/Woodroffe | Hours Daily 11am–7pm | Tip In 2009, Barack Obama bought cookies for his daughters at Le Moulin de Provence. "Obama Cookies," maple leaf-shaped shortbreads with red and white icing are still available (55 ByWard Market Square, www.lemoulindeprovence.com).

47___Hostel in a Jail

Come sleep on "death row"

When the Carleton County Gaol functioned from 1862 to 1972, its tiny cells lacked heating, lighting, toilets, ventilation and even beds in the early years. Conditions were inhumane. When Hostelling International took over the four-storey space, it left the gallows intact, created a death row interpretation centre and transformed the cells into private rooms when it opened August 2, 1973. "We turned the building into a living museum," says general manager Greg Brockmann. "We've set up displays around the property telling some of the historical stories. Every room has the name of somebody who was in the jail."

The imposing stone building was once connected by underground tunnel to a courthouse. Its most famous inmate was Patrick J. Whelan (see ch. 17), who was hanged before 5,000 people on February 11, 1869, for assassinating politician Thomas D'Arcy McGee in what was Canada's last public execution. Some suspect his remains were among those discovered when part of the site was excavated for the Mackenzie King Bridge. Paranormal investigators have studied the jail, and Haunted Walk Ottawa brings a tour here.

During COVID, the hostel was temporarily taken over by the city as a homeless shelter, and then rebranded as Saintlo Ottawa Jail Hostel. It's being refreshed and will reopen in 2023 but can always be admired from the outside. There are 80 modestly priced rooms. A few dorms have bunks to sleep four, six or eight people, and one family room sleeps six. Most of the rooms are former cells. Of five types of private rooms, the two most interesting are "authentic jail cells" that are just three feet by nine feet, and "historic double cells" in the former solitary confinement area. Guests can join free daily tours and borrow a Ouija board to contact restless spirits. Among the artifacts on display are old straightjackets and a letter an inmate wrote on toilet paper.

Address 75 Nicholas Street, Ottawa, ON K1N 7B9, +1 (613) 235-2595, www.saintlo.ca/en/ottawa-jail, ottawa@saintlo.ca | Getting there O-Train to Rideau (Line 1) | Hours Open 24 hours | Tip Four tombstones honour multiple people who died between 1882 and 1923. The grassy lot was once a Methodist church and most of its graves were relocated (northeast corner of Bank Street / Analdea Drive).

48 House of TARG
Perogies, pinball and live music

Pairing perogies with pinball doesn't make instant sense for a music venue, but it happened organically for House of TARG. It was 2014, and musician/producer Paul Granger rented his studio to bands in the punk community as a rehearsal space and held underground parties. At the same time, a friend dropped off a 1980 arcade game called TARG, and Granger got hooked on it. He decided to "do something legit" and, with Mark McHale and Kevin Berger, leased a 372-square-metre (4,000-square-foot) basement venue. They launched House of TARG on April 17, 2014, with a show by Canadian rock band PUP.

The focus soon morphed into music, perogies and games – games are social and a great way to kill time between bands. Because Granger is Ukrainian, they decided it would be fun to serve homemade perogies, not grasping that "it's so labour intensive it's almost impossible to make money off that." Still, they usually serve seven kinds, from the Traditional (potato and cheese) and Kale 'Em All (potato, roasted kale and smoked cheddar) to the Vegan with faux cheddar and bacon. All come with pickled beets, sauerkraut and dill-infused sour cream. Bacon and sautéed onions can be added.

The staff here call themselves "wizards." Pre-COVID, they'd sell up to 6,000 perogies a week, while hosting live music four nights a week and a Sunday DJ. Through COVID, TARG, with fourth partner Blake Jacobs, came to rely heavily on sales of fresh and frozen perogies and switched the games to $10 per person for unlimited, family-friendly play.

Look for around 19 pinball machines (*Star Wars*, *Ghostbusters*, *Kiss*), and up to 25 classic arcade games (*Police Trainer*, *Quick & Crash*, *Teenage Mutant Ninja Turtles*). Sadly for the nostalgics, the TARG machine is gone, but it inspired the logo: a swirl of planets, pinball machines and perogies. "It's not a very exciting game," Granger admits, "so it never really got much play."

Address 1077 Bank Street, Ottawa, ON K1S 3W9, +1 (613) 680-8274, www.houseoftarg.com | Getting there Bus 6, 7 to Bank/Aylmer | Hours Wed & Thu 5–11pm, Fri 5pm–2am, Sat & Sun 11–2am | Tip Momo Spot, Ottawa's first Nepalese eatery, serves steamed, pan-fried or deep-fried *momos*, dumplings filled with pork, chicken or vegetables (79 Holland Avenue, www.iwantmomos.com).

49 Igor Gouzenko Plaques
The Soviet defector who triggered the Cold War

Two plaques on the edge of an unassuming park honour the dramatic story of a Soviet intelligence officer and cipher clerk whose daring defection ushered in the Cold War. Igor Gouzenko was working at the Soviet Embassy in Ottawa, when he smuggled out 109 documents on September 5, 1945 (three days after the Japanese surrendered and World War II ended) that revealed that spies had infiltrated the government, the military and a lab that held atomic bomb secrets. At first, government officials and the *Ottawa Journal* didn't believe that the Soviets were spying on their war-time allies. Gouzenko, his pregnant wife Svetlana and infant son then defected and were sent to a safe house.

The signs are in Dundonald Park across from the red brick apartment building at 511 Somerset Street, where the family lived. This is the park where Royal Canadian Mounted Police spied on the family, not knowing they were actually hiding in a neighbour's apartment. Igor's documents led to the arrest of 39 suspects, the conviction of 18 of them and a Royal Commission, the Taschereau-Kellock Commission, that confirmed the Soviet spy ring's existence in Canada, the United States and the United Kingdom. Gouzenko's family received Canadian citizenship and new identities. He made occasional public and television appearances, famously wearing a white hood. He lived in fear near Toronto and his grave went unmarked for years until his wife died and was buried beside him.

In 2003, the city unveiled this photo panel commemorating the Gouzenko Affair. In 2004, the federal Historic Sites and Monuments Board added a plaque. Together they form a small but important memorial. *In our opinion Gouzenko, by what he has done, has rendered a great public service to the people of this country and has thereby placed Canada in his debt*, reads a quote on the sign from the Taschereau-Kellock Commission.

THE GOUZENKO AFFAIR
L'AFFAIRE GOUZENKO
1945-1946

The Gouzenko affair alerted the Canadian public to the Cold War. In September 1945, Igor Gouzenko, a cipher clerk at the Soviet embassy, revealed a network of documents to the United States and in Great Britain. His allegations led in 1946 to the creation of a royal Commission of inquiry known as the Kellock-Taschereau Commission. Its revelations of the country's vulnerability convinced the federal government to adopt measures to strengthen the national security system.

L'affaire Gouzenko fit prendre conscience à la population canadienne des différents enjeux de la Guerre froide. En septembre 1945, Igor Gouzenko, un commis au chiffre de l'ambassade soviétique à Ottawa, révèle un réseau de documents aux États-Unis et en Grande-Bretagne. Ses révélations mènent en 1946 à la création d'une commission royale d'enquête connue sous le nom de Commission Kellock-Taschereau. Sa mise en évidence de la vulnérabilité du pays convainquit le gouvernement canadien d'adopter des mesures pour renforcer la sécurité nationale.

Historic Sites and Monuments Board of Canada,
Commission des lieux et monuments historiques du Canada,
Government of Canada · Gouvernement du Canada

Address Dundonald Park, 516 Somerset Street, Ottawa, ON K1R 5J9, +1 (613) 580-2595, www.ottawa.ca | Getting there O-Train to Lyon (Line 1), then walk 10 minutes | Hours Unrestricted | Tip Ward 14 is a neighbourhood cocktail and beer bar "disguised as a consignment shop," with a tiny bottle shop/convenience store called The Dep (139 Preston Street, www.wardfourteen.com).

50__Interzip Rogers

Zip from Ontario to Quebec

The world's first interprovincial zipline lets thrill-seekers soar over the Ottawa River from Ontario to Quebec, taking in views of Parliament Hill and Chaudière Falls (see ch. 26). Just before Interzip debuted in June 2021, President Alex Van Dieren referred to the zipline as "the sixth link," inferring that the zipline would be joining five interprovincial bridges as a new crossing.

Riders start in Gatineau in the ticket office at Zibi's O Condominiums. Then it's a quick walk across Chaudière Bridge to the launch tower on Ottawa's Chaudière Island to put on helmets and harnesses and climb 120 feet. Riders sit in suspended seats with hands on overhead bars and knees pulled up for landing. There are two parallel cables and a "safety launch system" that won't let the top gate open until the rider ahead at the bottom is off the cable.

The ride clocks in at 40 kilometres an hour and lasts up to 40 seconds, depending on your weight. "You just let yourself go, and the system will do the rest," promises the Quebec-based Van Dieren. The idea came to the co-president of creative agency Orkestra several years after a ziplining experience in Costa Rica. "It has never been done in the world between two states, countries or provinces," he says.

Orkestra partnered with Zibi, a 34-acre, master-planned waterfront community that straddles Gatineau and Ottawa, for land for the two sites. The decision on which province to start in and which to end in was "an engineering decision," based on geography and topography. You can't zip with phones or cameras, but Interzip will sell you photos or a multi-angle video. All ages are welcome, and you must weigh between 70 and 275 pounds. At the base of the tower, stop to admire *Bimitigweyaa: The River Flows Along* by Anishinaabe artist Emily Kewageshig. The site-specific artwork acknowledges the Algonquin Anishinaabe land below the Interzip installation.

Address 40 Rue Jos-Montferrand, Gatineau, QC J8X 0C2, +1 (613) 695-5248, www.interzip.ca, info@interzip.ca | Getting there Bus 20, 22, 23, 24, 29 to Terasses de La Chaudière, then walk 6 minutes | Hours See website for seasonal hours | Tip For a Moroccan feast of *tajines* or couscous – sometimes with a belly dancer – Chez Fatima offers North African fare in downtown Gatineau (125 Promenade du Portage, Gatineau, www.chezfatima.ca).

51 Irving Rivers
Where souvenirs meet Canadiana

The poutine snow globe is popular at Irving River, as are the RCMP and Parliament Hill puzzles. Postcards and lapel pins never go out of style. Nor do keychains with beavers, moose and maple leaves. And people have an insatiable need for t-shirts. Same with socks, whether they sport a caricature of Prime Minister Justin Trudeau or are the thermal kind made in Canada of merino wool that keep you warm when it's 30 below. Flags – Pride, pansexual, genderqueer and more alongside provincial and international ones – sell like crazy. There are also customers devoted to the military side of things, like used combat pants and all things camo.

Baseball hats are a staple, but if you ask Ellen Rivers about toques, she'll say, "Toques, toques, toques, toques. Always toques. Toques are Canada. Everybody needs a toque, whether they're walking outside and forgot theirs at home, or whether they want a souvenir."

Irving Rivers was launched in 1950 by Ellen's dad, Irving Rivers, on a prime corner spot in ByWard Market, and the shop eventually expanded into two adjoining businesses. Thousands of items are packed into the "souvenir-plus" store that Ellen owns and her son Michael Osterer manages. Outside, under the slogan "We corner the market," is a tall stuffed moose that stands on his haunches and often looks quite dashing when he wears a red RCMP jacket or the popular "I am Canadian" t-shirts, that include phrases like, "I wear a toque not a fur hat." Ellen buys what sells and accommodates the most common customer requests.

By selling a little bit of everything, she says, "We hope that we can corner each market." She misses her dad, who died in 1997. "I'm so grateful that he started this and left a legacy for us to continue. I always say the store is not a person, but it has its own personality, and you have to be looking after it and nurturing it. I'm hoping that it's fun for people to come in."

Address 24 ByWard Market Square, Ottawa, ON K1N 7A2, +1 (613) 241-1415, www.irvingrivers.com, irvingrivers.24@gmail.com | **Getting there** O-Train to Rideau (Line 1) | **Hours** Mon–Fri 10am–4pm, Sat 10am–5pm, Sun noon–5pm | **Tip** Makers House Co. brings "the maker movement to main street retail." It sells things made by Canadian artisans and hosts events and workshops (987 Wellington Street W, www.makerhouse.com).

52 _Jean Richard_ Shipwreck

Remnants of a historic ship

Launched May 23, 1959, with great fanfare from Petite-Rivière, Quebec, the wooden ship _Jean Richard_ transported cargo for almost two decades on the St. Lawrence River and then enjoyed a second life as a river cruise/party ship called _Ville de Vanier_ that worked the Ottawa River in Gatineau. When police shut down the ship because of illegal gambling, it transformed once more into a floating cottage until catching fire while being moved for winter storage.

"Its charred, lifeless hulk was hauled off to rot in a concealed inlet off the Ottawa River, abandoned and left to decay into history where it now lies," reports CapitalGems.ca, a website run by those who explore the region's caves, mines and abandoned places. Today, you can hike along a creek to see the remains of the once-proud ship.

There's no plaque honouring what used to be a 36.5-metre (120-foot), flat-bottomed ship built by Philippe Lavoie for captain/carpenter Paul Émile Carré, but watch a 1963 National Film Board documentary by René Bonnière and Pierre Perrault called _The Jean Richard_ to see how Quebec sailors who doubled as craftsmen spent six months building it "in the form of the snow goose floating on the river," using tools and techniques with which "Noah must have built the ark." The film follows a village party and the celebratory launch, explaining how the local tradition was to name a new ship after the captain's son.

These wooden coastal freighters had short lives, leaking after a decade and usually being abandoned at beach graveyards after 20 years. The _Jean Richard_ was one of the last of its kind before larger steel ships took over. The wreck site, near the Voyageurs Pathway and Màwandòseg Bridge, a pedestrian/cyclist bridge previously called the Leamy Lake Discharge Bridge, isn't marked and can be hard to find. But you'll be able to view it up close or from the other side of the creek.

Address East side of Leamy Creek (off the Ottawa River), Gatineau, QC J8X 3P5 | Getting there Bus 867 to Bériault/Lambert, walk to Màwandòseg Bridge, then south on the footpath along the west side of the creek | Hours Unrestricted | Tip Try the slots at the government-run Casino du Lac-Leamy, or go for live music in its 1,100-seat theatre (1 Boulevard du Casino, Gatineau, https://casinos.lotoquebec.com).

53 Just Food Community Farm

Come to the market, take a food-themed stroll

Every Sunday from spring to fall, and sporadic Sundays through the winter, multiple vendors from Just Food Community Farm set up a market stand that's bursting with fresh produce and other home-grown treats. Sometimes it's located right at the farm gate, and other times it's in the big red barn. This is the place to come to load up on garlic, tomatoes, carrots, squash, greens and more. Or maybe it's local honey and preserves you crave. Visiting the weekly farm stand is the easiest entry point to the multi-faceted Just Food world.

Started in 2012, the grassroots, non-profit Just Food Community Farm leases 150 acres of National Capital Commission Greenbelt land just west of Blackburn Hamlet. The group's three-part focus is on education, demonstrations and training. There are always scores of projects and people on site. A nine-acre Community Food Forest is bursting with hundreds of things that people can eat and boasts nut trees, berry bushes and sap trees. There's an incubator farm for new farmers, workshops, food conferences and culinary events. You can attend demonstrations about everything from sustainable energy to food and housing. There's a teaching greenhouse, children's programming, plant-a-row, grow-a-row gardens and growing space for new Canadians.

"People can walk around on the site to enjoy seeing the connection between food and nature," says Just Food's executive director Moe Garahan. "There are a lot of trees, ravines and pathways. People are welcome to walk with their families and come and eat on site." The farm is gated but is usually unlocked between early morning and early evening to welcome visitors. There are plans afoot for better interpretive signage and guided tours. A new pavilion will likely house the Sunday market, which plans to start featuring local chefs using the ingredients to cook and sell breakfast.

Address 2391 Pépin Court, Ottawa, ON K1B 4Z3, +1 (613) 824-7771, https://justfood.ca/
just-food-farm, info@justfood.ca | Getting there O-Train to Blair (Line 1), then bus 25 to
Innes/Tauvette | Hours See website | Tip Vignoble Clos du Vully grows cold climate grapes.
An old dairy barn doubles as winery, and wine store and private tastings can be booked
(2501 Magladry Road, www.vignobleclosduvully.com).

54 Le Cordon Bleu Ottawa
A taste of France

Ottawa is home to the only North American campus for the world-renowned Le Cordon Bleu, the guardian of French culinary techniques. Food lovers come to study culinary arts and hospitality management, taking elaborate diploma programs or gourmet classes.

As the official Cordon Bleu story goes, knights of France's prestigious Order of the Holy Spirit, established in 1579, wore cross pendants hanging from blue ribbons and were known as "Cordons Bleus." Thanks to their lavish meals, the term "cordon bleu" soon became synonymous with culinary excellence. Le Cordon Bleu cooking school debuted in Paris in 1895. International alumni include Julia Child, Yotam Ottolenghi, and Mary Berry.

So how did a campus wind up in Ottawa? In 1979, Ottawa's Eleanor Orser became the school's first Canadian graduate after earning her *Grand Diplôme* in Paris. The women from her husband's accounting firm wanted to know what she learned, and so she created Eleanor's Cuisine Française on Prince of Wales Drive and began teaching. In 1988, she sold the school to Le Cordon Bleu, and it became the first campus outside of Europe during an international expansion.

In a 1988 *Ottawa Citizen* article about the sale, company president André Cointreau called the bilingual city "culturally interesting" and expected to draw students from Montreal, Toronto and New York. He kept on Orser to uphold the standards. As she told the paper, "Once you learn to cook the French way, you will never sit down to a mediocre meal again."

In 2000, the school moved to the historic Munross mansion, built in 1874 by Scottish lumberman James Mather. The Sandy Hill school has teaching classrooms and Signatures Restaurant, run by chef Yannick Anton and popular with the diplomatic community. Ottawa's is now one of 35 campuses in 20 countries that together train more than 20,000 students per year.

Address 453 Laurier Avenue East, Ottawa, ON K1N 6R4, +1 (613) 236-2433, www.cordonbleu.edu/ottawa, ottawa@cordonbleu.edu | Getting there Bus 19 to Laurier E/Range | Hours See website | Tip C'est Bon Cooking, co-owned by Georges Laurier and Stefanie Siska' hosts cooking classes, gourmet food tours through the National Capital Region and team-building experiences (200 Dalhousie Street, Ottawa, www.cestboncooking.ca).

55 Lime Kiln Ruins

Signs of early industrial heritage

The ruins of one of Canada's last remaining 19th-century industrial lime kilns can be found in a forest down a short, family-friendly trail in Stony Swamp. Lime is a key building and household chemical used to make products like mortar, fertilizer, whitewash and plaster. Francis Flood, about whom we know very little, built this kiln in the late 1800s on a miniature escarpment of exposed limestone bedrock known as the Hazeldean Fault.

Most lime producers went out of business in the early 1900s, as new and larger industrial kilns were constructed and Portland cement was introduced from Europe. *The Flood kiln ceased operation around 1906, and the site was abandoned and fell into disrepair*, says an aging National Capital Commission interpretive panel. *The ruins of the kiln were rediscovered and its significance realized in the early 1970s. The site was restored in 1999.*

The lime produced here was sold to local industries, and farmers and settlers used it to make mortar for "chinking" log houses and grouting stone houses. The area once had five outbuildings built around a circular kiln pot, including a powder magazine to store black powder for quarrying and a Limehouse to store finished lime. Wood and limestone were sourced from the nearby escarpment, put in the kiln pot and fired for several days. That created ash and lime that was then removed from an opening at the bottom of the kiln and stored in another building.

The Canadian Lime Institute says lime has been produced here since the 1600s and is one of the country's founding industries. It's now produced using modern and efficient technology, and it remains an integral part of the Canadian economy. These ruins boast just a few explanatory signs, with sketches and archival photos. You'll wander among crumbling stone buildings spread out in the greenery. Look for a grate over what was once the kiln pot.

Address Lime Kiln Trail, NCC Greenbelt Parking Lot P10, Ottawa, ON K2R 1H3, www.ncc-ccn.gc.ca | **Getting there** By car, take Trans-Canada Highway (Highway 417 W) to Nepean, then Exit 72 to Highway 416 S, then West Hunt Club Road / Ottawa 32, then south on Regional Road 11 to the parking lot and trailhead | **Hours** Daily 7am–10pm | **Tip** Jack Pine Trail, also in the Stony Swamp Conservation Area, has three loops, crosses beaver ponds and is a good place for cross-country skiing and snowshoeing in winter (from parking lot P9, www.ncc-ccn.gc.ca).

56 _ Lord Stanley's Gift
Hockey's hold on Canadian identity

Hockey fans jonesing to see – or somehow touch – the sport's top trophy can have a moment with a Stanley Cup monument on the Sparks Street Mall at Elgin Street. Lord Stanley's Gift Monument is inspired by the simple silver bowl donated by Lord Frederick Stanley of Preston in 1892, when he was Canada's sixth governor general and a hockey fan who wanted to celebrate "the champion hockey team in the Dominion." Stanley donated the cup on March 18, 1892, at a season-ending banquet at the Russell House Hotel (now Confederation Square).

The sculptural installation – with views of Confederation Square – starts with a 3.45-metre-high (11.3-foot) chalice made of silvered aluminum bands that people can walk through on two sides. It rises from a patch of pavement modified to resemble a white, paved hockey rink. Look for the stainless-steel lines that resemble skate marks and the 39 granite discs engraved with the names of Stanley Cup winners from 1893 to 2017. A black granite bench shaped like a hockey puck completes the compact space. The design is the work of artist Linda Covit, landscape architect Bao-Chau Nguyen and senior design architect/associate Joseph Moro of the NORR architectural firm.

"Hockey looms large in our collective consciousness, and the Stanley Cup is one of its most powerful symbols," said Mélanie Joly when she was Minister of Canadian Heritage in 2017 as the monument was unveiled to mark the 150th anniversary of Confederation, the centennial of the National Hockey League and the 125th anniversary of Stanley's gift. George Hunter, vice-president and chair of the non-profit Lord Stanley Memorial Monument Inc., called the Stanley Cup a "modest cup that grew up to be the world's most sought-after hockey trophy, hockey's holy grail." The monument, he pointed out, "magnifies and abstracts" the Stanley Cup's "original, modest form."

Address 59 Sparks Street, Ottawa, ON K1P 6E4 | Getting there O-Train to Parliament (Line 1) | Hours Unrestricted | Tip On a bronze statue of hockey legend Maurice "Rocket" Richard of Montreal Canadiens fame, his motto "Never give up" is etched into the base in English and French (Jacques Cartier Park, Gatineau, www.ncc-ccn.gc.ca/places/jacques-cartier-park).

57 Love Locks
Romantic gestures on the Corktown Footbridge

Sweethearts looking to make public declarations of love gravitate to the Corktown Footbridge to add their personalized "love locks" to the modest collection attached to the railings. The locks – mostly padlocks, with some combination types – are painted with names, initials and loving thoughts. Keys are tossed into the Rideau Canal for good luck. But nothing lasts forever, especially urban love locks.

"Earlier this week, 'love locks' on the Corktown Footbridge were removed due to the amount, placement and clumping of locks," warned one 2019 tweet by the City of Ottawa. "Staff regularly inspect the bridge and remove damaged chains and padlocks, but residents can continue to place new 'love locks' on the bridge."

No one knows when or where the tradition began. It was popularized by the late-2000s Italian book / film *Ho Voglia di Te* (*I Want You*), which has a love lock scene at Rome's Ponte Milvio. Paris famously drew amorous tourists to its historic Pont des Arts bridge over the Seine until the bridge started to collapse under the weight of more than 700,000 locks. That threat, combined with illegal and cheap lock peddlers, pickpockets, graffiti and the No Love Locks advocacy group who call the tradition "a modern plague on Paris," hastened a massive lock removal blitz and the installation of clear glass panels. The trend has died down significantly.

The Passerelle Corktown Footbridge opened in 2007. The name speaks to the fact that many unsung Irish labourers built the Rideau Canal (see ch. 22) and lived in a west bank encampment called "Corkstown" after Ireland's County Cork. The footbridge links the Golden Triangle at Somerset Street West to the University of Ottawa. Not to put a damper on love, but while it may be romantic to toss keys into the water to signify an everlasting bond, the decaying keys are bad for the environment. So, take your key with you.

Address Rideau Canal at Somerset Street W, Ottawa, ON | Getting there O-Train to uOttawa (Line 1) | Hours Unrestricted | Tip Scramble over the rocks and enjoy the vistas of the Prince of Wales Falls / Hog's Bag Falls at Hog's Back Park, a series of artificial waterfalls at the Rideau Canal / Rideau River split (www.ncc-ccn.gc.ca/places/hogs-back-park).

58 M&G's Chipwagon

365 days of French fries

Fried potatoes in any form are loved around the world. *Poutine*, fries smothered in beef gravy and squeaky cheese curds, is a Quebec creation that has devotees across the country and beyond. But chip trucks? They're an old-school Ontario thing.

Long before modern-day food trucks arrived on the scene, with their fancy kitchens, trendy dishes and clever branding, we'd see unapologetically battered chips trucks, trailers or stands on the side of the road, often in the corner of a parking lot, dishing out a seemingly endless supply of fries. These are vehicles that have wheels but never move.

The M&G's Chipwagon is a bright yellow chip truck that hasn't changed a bit since Akel Zahalan launched it at the corner of Bank Street and Sunnyside Avenue in 1991. He put his four kids through school with the proceeds from this business, after leaving a job as a chef at the House of Commons and renting the parking lot space from someone who hails from Lebanon like he does. Most chip trucks are seasonal, fair-weather creatures that make their money through the warmer weather and then shut down for winter. But M&G's Chipwagon shrugs off the rain, the snow and the city's famously windy and sub-zero temperatures to stay open 365 days of the year. Being so close to Quebec, it's no surprise that poutine (not plain fries) is listed first on the menu.

This late-night haunt for drinkers and revellers is weirdly loved for its often terse service. Yelp reviewers have called the truck "the devil that lives down the street" and argued over whether it's the best or worst poutine in Ottawa. What they often forget is that this is "drunk food" – the thing you crave during a wild night out. In a 2008 Yelp review, Sarah G. waxed poetic, "M&G is to poutine what the Louvre is to art, what Meryl Streep is to Hollywood, what Spam is to other canned meats. It is one of a kind and original."

Address 1089 Bank Street at Sunnyside Avenue, Ottawa, ON K1S 3W9 | Getting there Bus 6, 7 to Bank/Aylmer | Hours Daily from 10:30am | Tip Carleton University boasts five kilometres (three miles) of tunnels built in the 1960s that everyone uses to travel between campus buildings (1125 Colonel By Drive, www.carleton.ca).

59 Macdonald Gardens

The park that was once a cemetery

It may sound like an urban legend, but bodies really are still buried in Macdonald Gardens, the Lowertown East park that was one of the city's earliest cemeteries. Between 1845 and 1873, the Episcopalian, Presbyterian, Wesleyan Methodist and Roman Catholic churches operated Sandy Hill Cemeteries in what was then called Bytown. They divided the rectangular space into four cemeteries, according to a portion of an 1839 plan that's posted by the southern entrance.

"When Sandy Hill Cemeteries closed, families of the deceased were asked to claim and move the remains," according to a 2014 community heritage report about the neighbourhood done by Carleton University graduate students at the School of Canadian Studies. "However, many of the families could not afford to move them, did not want to, had moved out of the area or were no longer surviving." From 1873 to 1909, "a number of remains" were moved to the new Beechwood and Notre-Dame cemeteries, according to the signage at the Tormey Street/Charlotte Street entrance. In 1911, the inscriptions of the remaining headstones were read aloud in City Council.

In 1912, the Ottawa Improvement Commission (now the National Capital Commission) began creating a public park on the site and covered over the remaining graves. Newspaper reports have detailed unclaimed human remains being left behind and the 1936 discovery of a skull in the park.

The park was named for Canada's first prime minister, Sir John A. Macdonald, but locals dubbed it Borden Park after another prime minister, Sir Robert Borden, who lived across from it. Designed by one of the founders of Canada's landscape architect movement, Frederick G. Todd, Macdonald Gardens opened in 1914. Now a protected heritage space, it has open green areas, tree-lined paths and the gazebo-like stone "summer house" on a grassy hill that has views of Parliament Hill. It's nicknamed "Hill of Bones."

Address 99 Cobourg Street, Ottawa, ON K1N 5Z7 | Getting there Bus 7, 19 to Cobourg/Beausoleil | Hours Daily 5am–11pm | Tip The Embassy of the Republic of Turkey was the site of a 1985 attack by Armenian revolutionaries that took hostages and killed a guard (197 Wurtemburg Street, http://ottava.be.mfa.gov.tr/Mission).

60 Mādahòkì Farm

Home to rare Ojibwe spirit horses

Their names are Makwa (Black Bear), Mukaday-Wagoosh (Black Fox), Migizi (Eagle), Gwiingwiishi (Grey Jay) and Kitagokons (Fawn / Young Deer). They are some of the rare Ojibwe spirit horses that now have a permanent home at Mādahòkì Farm in western Ottawa's Greenbelt. The breed pre-dates the arrival of European settlers to this continent, cultural ambassador Maggie Downer explains after detailing the importance of the fire pit and performing a song.

The farm is the creation of Indigenous Experiences, a group that has long produced the annual Summer Solstice Indigenous Festival and runs an attraction at the Canadian Museum of History. It provides agritourism, farm-to-table culinary experiences and cultural experiences from an Indigenous perspective. There are festivals to celebrate the four seasons with performances, workshops and meals, and a year-round Indigenous marketplace that promotes the creations of 40 Indigenous artists, makers, farmers and businesses. A walking trail through the forest details traditional plants, explains Trina Mather-Simard, the executive and artistic director.

Mādahòkì Farm is on the traditional unceded territory of the Algonquin Nation. The name means "to share the land" in the Anishinaabe language and is pronounced Mu-dah-o-key. Indigenous Experiences leases from property stewards, the National Capital Commission. Not only is this a safe space where Indigenous communities can reconnect with the land through healing and wellness programs and social enterprise opportunities, it's a gathering place for working towards greater understanding and reconciliation with all Canadians through sharing the traditional teachings and gifts of the land from an Indigenous perspective. The goal is to promote Indigenous food sovereignty by farming traditional agricultural foods, and eventually bison and elk, with farm-to-table experiences.

Address 4420 West Hunt Club Road, Nepean, ON K2R 1H4, www.indigenous-experiences.ca/madahoki-farm, madahoki@indigenous-experiences.ca | **Getting there** By car, take ON-416 S to exit 72 toward Nepean, and turn right onto W Hunt Club Road/Ottawa 32. Location will be on the right. | **Hours** See website | **Tip** Skate through an urban forest with Icelynd Skating Trails or rent its outdoor rink for your own hockey games. It's co-owned by former Ottawa Senators winger Chris Neil (6865 Fernbank Road, Stittsville, www.icelynd.com).

61 Maple Hill Urban Farm
Take an alpaca for a walk

At Maple Hill Urban Farm in the city's west end, Don Trott's animals must "have a use" and be people friendly. That's because he invites the public to visit with the chickens, goats and pigs, buy garlic and vegetables from his allotment garden farmers, and take the alpacas and "lalpacas" (llama / alpaca crosses) for guided walks. The 45-minute walks start with an overview on the animals, followed by a leashed romp around the property, a visit with the other barnyard residents and finally a stop at the shop selling honey, eggs and alpaca products, like socks, hats and scarves.

Alpacas, Trott admits, "are not exactly touchy, feeling animals, like a dog – but they tolerate us, and they pick up on your energy quite easily." He and another guide can handle up to a dozen walks a week (each is for groups of up to four people that arrive together), but the numbers ebb and flow, depending on the season and whether school's in session. You can give feed to the alpacas, and you can also bring greens for them as a treat.

The 167-acre farm is in the Greenbelt, a publicly owned swath of land that includes wetlands, farmlands and forests. In 2012, the farm was leased as part of the National Capital Commission's sustainable farmland program. Trott has also been hosting a popular corn maze in the fall ever since. He came to alpacas in 2016 after his friendly llama died (as guard animals, they can be mean) and he sold his horses. "It's like an empty closet – you've got to fill it." Alpacas are flight animals and enjoy safety in numbers, so he expanded the herd in 2021 and usually has about six.

Trott rents land to about 130 farmers, who mainly tend to family gardens. Some are immigrants from places like Syria and Cameroon. "We want to focus more on growing food than entertainment," says Trott, "but people really like coming out and seeing the animals, so I like that too."

Address 200 Moodie Drive, Ottawa, ON K2H 8K6, +1 (613) 828-2987, www.maplehillurbanfarm.com, maplehillurbanfarm@gmail.com | **Getting there** Bus 57 to Fitzgerald/A.D. 16, then walk 15 minutes | **Hours** By reservation only | **Tip** Captiva Farms offers Western-style trail rides year-round in rain and snow, but not in "extreme weather" (189 Chemin de la Montagne, Wakefield, www.captivafarms.com).

62 Maplelawn Garden

It's all about the historical walls

The early 19th century was a heyday for fine Ontario houses, but only some boasted walled gardens, and precious few have survived across Canada. Maplelawn House and Garden in Westboro was designated a national historic site in 1989 for being "a rare and well-preserved example of a country estate," with a walled garden. It is cared for by the National Capital Commission (NCC) and a volunteer group called the Friends of Maplelawn Garden that studies, preserves and rejuvenates the grounds. According to Heritage Ottawa, the house was "once part of a large prosperous farm" on the outskirts of town and has links to three important early local families.

The 2.5-storey stone house was built in the British classical tradition 1831 to 1834 for Scottish farmer William Thomson. The rectangular kitchen garden was enclosed on three sides by "uncoursed random rubble boundary walls" to grow vegetables, fruit and flowers. Lumberman Thomas Cole later turned the property into a dairy farm and eventually sold it to his son John, who electrified the farm and subdivided the land into a new neighbourhood. Lloyd B. Rochester bought the property in 1935, renamed it Maplelawn and hired landscape architect R. Warren Oliver to renew the garden as a lush, ornamental perennial space.

The house is now leased to The Keg Steakhouse as the Ottawa Manor, but the nearly one-acre symmetrical garden with "rough-dressed limestone walls" welcomes the public. The NCC says that together they "reveal how European architectural and landscape ideals were transplanted to Canada." But the big draw is the serenity of the garden. An extensive array of plants – everything from Climbing Rose and Creeping Phlox to Mock Orange and Tiger Lilies – has been chosen based on historical and developmental documents. One rarity is flower-of-an-hour (*Hibiscus trionum*), which blooms for just one hour each year.

Address 529 Richmond Street, Ottawa, ON K2A 0G3, +1 (613) 239-5000, www.ncc-ccn.gc.ca/places/maplelawn-garden | Getting there Bus 11 to Richmond/ Broadview | Hours Apr–Oct daily dawn–dusk | Tip Billings Estate Museum National Historic Site, the city's oldest wood-framed house, belonged to a prosperous early settler. Its community cemetery has graves of pioneers (2100 Cabot Street, www.ottawa.ca).

63 Margaret Atwood's Key
Birthing a literary icon

A small photo of Canadian literary icon Margaret Atwood hangs on the wall of Ottawa City Hall. If you're wondering why the Torontonian, who wrote books like *The Handmaid's Tale*, *The Robber Bride* and *Alias Grace*, has been feted in a display for the "Key to the City of Ottawa Recipients," it's because she was born at Ottawa General Hospital on November 18, 1939.

Atwood spent some of her early years in the Glebe (at 314 First Avenue) and soon moved to a second-storey apartment at 1 Patterson Avenue by the Rideau Canal before the family relocated to Sault Ste. Marie in 1945. Her entomologist dad studied insects, so Atwood once told *The New York Times* she grew up "in and out of the bush." The family eventually settled in Toronto, where Atwood still lives.

"The Key of Ottawa is entrusted to those whom the city would honour, as a symbol of our hope that the recipient is so regarded as being of the very household of our municipal life that he or she may be expected to return to Ottawa and be freely, fully and fondly welcome at all times as a citizen loving and loved, of this city," reads a framed 1956 explanation of the honour by then Mayor Charlotte Whitton. Also in the frame is a gold key. The people who have been honoured since 1936 are detailed in lists that have also been framed. You'll notice plenty of people with the words "Sir," "His Worship" and "His Excellency" before their names, but you'll also see artists and celebrities, like actor Paul Anka (1972), singer Bryan Adams (1998), actor Sandra Oh (2012) and game show host Alex Trebek of *Jeopardy* fame (2016).

The photo of Atwood shows her beaming as she accepts her key from Deputy Mayor Allan Higdon on September 20, 2000. She returns to Ottawa occasionally for fundraisers, festivals and literary events. Fans wander by the two addresses where Atwood once lived, but you won't find any plaques marking the sites.

Address 110 Laurier Avenue W, Ottawa, ON K1P 1J1 | Getting there O-Train to Parliament (Line 1), then walk 13 minutes | Hours Mon–Fri 9am–5pm | Tip The Ottawa Sport Hall of Fame celebrates top sporting moments through artifacts, photos and memorabilia (110 Laurier Avenue W, Lisgar Street entrance, www.ottawasporthalloffame.ca).

64 Mayfair Theatre

Loyal patrons got urinal naming rights

After the COVID lockdowns began in 2020, the Mayfair Theatre started selling naming rights to its 325 seats as a fundraiser. Then they moved on to movie poster boxes, emergency exits, couches, the projector, the balcony, the popcorn machine and more. But the surprise hit was the chance to attach your name to three urinals, one men's room stall and three women's washroom stalls. Glenn Hümplik, co-host of the cult TV hit *The Tom Green Show*, scored one urinal for $150, cheekily telling a Twitter user, "All I ask is you aim well."

Mayfair co-owner Josh Stafford says that even before the nameplates were added, the cramped washrooms had personality. Both have vintage *ladies* and *gents* stained-glass window signs. Heart-throbs Burt Reynolds and James Dean make poster appearances for the women. *The Shining*'s Jack Nicholson looms large for the men. "I think it's hilarious that we put the naming rights on the urinals and people bought 'em up very fast," Stafford admits, adding there's room for a name and a short saying on the nameplates.

The Mayfair is Ottawa's oldest active movie theatre. The independent repertory cinema has just one screen and runs indie, second-run and classic films, like *The Rocky Horror Picture Show* and *The Room*. Its ordinary exterior hides a vintage interior that the city protected with a heritage designation in 2008. The theatre, opened in 1932, was designed in the Spanish Colonial Revival style, which was quite popular in the first part of the 20th century. As you enter the auditorium, you'll notice that it both looks and feels like a Mediterranean plaza, which was the intent of designer René de Vos. Look for the details throughout, from the ceiling and the balconies to the wrought ironwork and the façades. The Mayfair Theatre is the last remaining building of this type. Don't miss the original auditorium clock, from the era when parents would simply drop off and pick up their kids.

Address 1074 Bank Street, Ottawa, ON K1S 3X3, +1 (613) 730-3403, www.mayfairtheatre.ca | Getting there Bus 6/7 to Bank/Sunnyside | Hours Daily, see website for showtimes | Tip Black Squirrel Books & Espresso Bar has food and drinks, plus live music, deejays and stand-up comedy events (1073 Bank Street, www.blacksquirrelbooks.ca).

65 Mer Bleue Bog Trail
Boardwalk through a mysterious ecosystem

Named by French settlers, Mer Bleue means "blue sea." Sometimes, if you arrive early enough on a day when mist rises over the bog, the area does, in fact, look like an immense blue sea. This magical bog is one of five types of wetlands, habitats where the land is wet for a period of time each year. About 10 kilometres (6 miles) from downtown, the sprawling Mer Bleue Conservation Area has four parking lots to accommodate visitors. It's best to start at the family-friendly Mer Bleue Bog Trail and meander along the short, universally accessible boardwalk to get the full story from a series of interpretive signs.

A relic of the Ice Age, Mer Bleue is a remarkable reflection of our northern landscape: vast, fragile and mysterious, reads one sign. This area is mainly a huge acidic peat bog with marshes and sand ridges poking out. Peat is not firm ground but "a buoyant mattress composed of moss." Besides being the largest bog (a type of peatland) and natural area in Canada's Capital Region and the second-largest bog in southern Ontario, Mer Bleue is a wetland of international significance under the Ramsar Convention of Wetlands.

People come to hike, bird-watch, take photos, cross-country ski and snowshoe. The National Capital Commission, which manages the region's 20,000-hectare Greenbelt, says Mer Bleue helps stabilize the climate and hosts a permanent research station that measures the amount of carbon dioxide and methane that's released by the wetland. There's a black spruce forest and open heath vegetation with low-lying and dwarf shrubs, including sphagnum moss, Labrador tea rhododendrons and sheep laurel. The area is humid, and decomposition happens slowly.

Look for beaver, moose, painted turtles, green frogs and American bitterns, and carnivorous plants, like pitcher plants, sundews and butterworts. Or just enjoy the peaceful stroll.

Address NCC Greenbelt parking lot P22, 5063 Ridge Road, Ramsayville, ON K0A 2Y0, www.ncc-ccn.gc.ca/places/mer-bleue | Getting there By car, take the Trans-Canada Highway / ON 417 E to exit 104 to Anderson Road. Regional Road 74 E, then turn right onto Ridge Road to destination / trailhead on the left. | Hours Daily 8am – sunset (9pm in summer) | Tip Park on Brookridge Crescent and walk through the woods down to Princess Louise Falls, a spectacular, natural waterfall in Orleans (just off St. Joseph Boulevard near 1st Avenue).

66 Mickle Macks Haberdashery

The joy of a jaunty hat

"Many a mickle makes a muckle" is a Scottish proverb that means "many small amounts accumulate to make a large amount." For Gina Csiffary, the saying is about "making small things add up to big things." It's a reminder of a revelatory birthday trip she took to Scotland with her husband, as she realized "climbing ladders was getting dull." She wanted to be her own boss. She also knew the biggest retail hole in Ottawa was hats, because she was constantly trying to buy them online and having to return them when they didn't fit properly. Mickle Macks Haberdashery, "a shop that's full of all the little things that make you happy." was born in late 2018."

"It's a small thing to have a nice hat," Csiffary says, "but it's a game-changer as far as a crappy day goes." She proudly sells hats that other people have made. There are many fedoras, a three-season hat that's typically made of wool or straw. One standout is the unisex Gord Downie fedora, created for the late lead singer of the Tragically Hip by Karyn Ruiz of Toronto's Lilliput Hats. There are colourful wool berets and hats by Nick Fouquet, milliner to Hollywood stars. You'll find sheepskin shearling aviator hats and rabbit trapper hats. Toques made of ethically sourced Mongolian cashmere are another highlight because of a Fair Trade agreement that channels funds from Mickle Macks through a chamber of commerce and directly to women artisans.

And Mickle Macks sells more than hats. There are socks, slippers, bathrobes, ties/bowties, cashmere scarves, ear warmers and all kinds of "soft, squishable, packable, giftable" things. Csiffary is wild about Thermohair socks made from kid mohar in South Mountain, not far from Ottawa. She and her staff let people explore the shop and then regale them with the stories behind the things that catch their eye. "My shop is full of thing that I want to have," admits Csiffary.

Address 835 Bank Street, Ottawa, ON K1S 3V9, +1 (613) 231-7222, www.micklemacks.com, sales@micklemacks.com | **Getting there** Bus 6, 7 to Bank/Fifth | **Hours** Tue–Fr 10am–6pm, Sat 10am–4pm, Sun 11am–4pm | **Tip** Crosstown Traffic is a counterculture variety store with pipes, vaporizers, bongs, cannabis paraphernalia, vinyl, DVDs, books and curiosities (593-C Bank Street, www.crosstowntraffic.shop).

67 Minto Bridges
Truss bridges beg to be photographed

Heritage bridge aficionados love this unusual trio. Minto Bridges are actually a set of three white bridges along Union Street that connects two small islands, Green and Maple, to neighbourhoods on either side of the Rideau River. From the North, a single span truss bridge links New Edinburgh to Maple Island. A two-span truss bridge then connects Maple Island to Green Island, the former home of Ottawa City Hall and now the federal Department of Foreign Affairs. Finally, a single span truss bridge connects Green Island to Lowertown at King Edward Avenue.

The ornate bridges were constructed between 1900 and 1902 as a grand processional route from Rideau Hall to Parliament Hill. They were made of lightweight steel sections and cast iron and erected under the direction of city engineer Robert Surtees for what was then called the Ottawa Improvement Commission. Prime Minister Wilfred Laurier set up the commission with an eye towards making Ottawa as beautiful as Washington, DC. The bridges were named after the 4th Earl of Minto, who was the eighth governor general of Canada between 1898 and 1904. He and his wife were reportedly interested in heritage, so it is a fitting tribute.

According to HistoricBridges.org, the Minto Bridges feature an early North American example of riveted connections instead of pin connections. They're ornately decorated in detailed portal cresting and finials and are notable for stunning pedestrian sidewalk railings in a rare arch lattice design.

The city recently had these "jewels of the Rideau River" restored, replacing a steel grate deck corroded by winter salt, and making the bridges stronger so fire trucks can cross. The city honoured the project team with an Ottawa Heritage Award for bringing "these magnificent bridges back to their original splendour." The bridges are used by motorists, cyclists and pedestrians and loved by photographers.

Address Union Street south of Stanley Avenue to north of King Edward Avenue, Ottawa, ON | Getting there Bus 9 (direction Hurdman) to Sussex / Rideau Falls | Hours Unrestricted | Tip Clothes Encounters of a Second Time is a consignment store that was founded to provide clothing to Vietnamese boat people and still donates to new communities (67 Beechwood Avenue, www.clothesencounters.ca).

68 _Mōnz_

Canal bench with Indigenous message

Public benches don't get much love, but _Mōnz_ (_Moose_) is the 2019 work of art by Algonquin artist Claude Latour and worth special attention. It's beside the Rideau Canal Western Pathway, by the lily pond and just steps north of the Flora Footbridge. The eye-catching bench, made from steel painted white and a wooden seat, emulates abstract moose antlers. It does double duty as a resting place for passersby and as public art signifying that the traditional territory of the Algonquin people has always included the Ottawa Valley and adjacent land in Ontario and Quebec.

The Ottawa-based Latour is a band member of the Kitigan Zibi Anishinabeg First Nation of Maniwaki, Quebec. As the trilingual _Mōnz_ plaque states, _Ottawa is built on unceded Algonquin Anishinaabe territory. [Latour] was inspired by the disturbance of the Rideau Canal. This disturbance caused the displacement of many animals including the moose._ Algonquin people have an ongoing relationship with the moose and once considered it essential for clothing and food. _This bench honours the past, present and future of the Algonquin People on whose unceded lands the Rideau Canal is built upon_, the plaque explains.

Nearby, the Flora Footbridge, which spans the canal, debuted in June 2019 to connect Clegg Street in Old Ottawa East to Fifth Avenue at Queen Elizabeth Drive in the Glebe. It was named after the late Flora MacDonald, who in 1976 became the second woman in Canadian history to make a serious run at the leadership of a major federal party (the Conservatives) and then became Canada's first female foreign minister in 1979.

On the east side of the footbridge, at the foot of the staircase ramp, look for a wood, steel and stone bench by Sally Lee Sheek called _Alone_. Like Latour, she was one of the emerging artists that submitted an expression of interest to the city for this unique public art commission.

Address Near Flora Footbridge, 467 Echo Drive, Ottawa, ON K1N 1N7 | **Getting there** Bus 5, 55 (direction Elmvale) to Main / Clegg, then walk towards the Rideau Canal | **Hours** Unrestricted | **Tip** The Overbrook Community Centre has two whimsical outdoor benches named *Connections* and created by sculptor-artist-blacksmith Cairn Cunnane from collected and fabricated steel (33 Quill Street).

69 Moo Shu Ice Cream

Clever flavours from a living wage employer

"I guess the theme of the store is things I would eat all the time," admits Liz Mok, owner of Moo Shu Ice Cream & Kitchen. The small batch scoopery offers creative flavours, vegan options and handmade waffles cones.

The Hong Kong-born Mok was raised in Greater Vancouver and schooled in industrial design at Ottawa's Carleton University. She yearned to turn her love of food into a career and in the summer of 2015, with help from partner Chris Mack, she sold ice cream at a farmer's market. The next year, she opened the 700-square-foot Moo Shu. The name was inspired by moo shu pork, a North American dish that baffled her family until they found it had ties to Shandong province and understood how it speaks to the immigrant experience and themes of survival and acceptance. The store name also references Mushu, the Chinese dragon in *Mulan*. "Obviously the cute part is that I get to put the word 'moo' in it," says Mok, who uses Ontario milk and cream for regular ice cream, and homemade oat milk blended with coconut milk for vegan options.

Everything revolves around local farm ingredients or Asian-inspired flavours. Hong Kong Milk Tea (strongly steeped red and black tea with evaporated milk) is the bestseller. For Local Strawberry, Mok buys, preps and freezes enough summer berries to last all year. White Rabbit (condensed milk and butter) riffs off the iconic Chinese candy. Monthly feature flavours are inspired by events, festivals, pop culture, Asian ingredients and whatever is in season. Ice cream sandwiches, dip bars and ice cream tacos are on offer alongside homemade frozen dumplings.

Moo Shu became a certified Living Wage employer after Mok appraised her company and the food industry. Her hourly wages are at least $3.60 above minimum wage. Price increases are offset by free regular cake cones and a scoop bank, where anyone can donate or claim a free scoop.

Address 477 Bank Street, Ottawa, ON K2P 1Z2, +1 (613) 565-1524, www.mooshuicecream.com, mooshuicecream@gmail.com | Getting there Bus 6, 7, 14 to Gladstone / Bank | Hours Wed – Thu 3 – 9pm, Fri – Sun noon – 9pm | Tip Dao Café has earned a following for its Evil Garlic Bun, specialty croissants, like the Thai milk tea flavour, and "sandos," or Japanese fruit sandwiches made on soft white bread (1558 Merivale Road, Unit 102, www.daocanada.com).

70—Morse Code Windows
Canadian War Museum sends secret message

From a distance, you can see an intriguing copper "fin" dotted with small, odd-shaped windows jutting out of the Canadian War Museum's northeast corner. They're not just windows, though, but a Morse Code message that spells out "Lest we forget" in English and "N'oublions jamais" in French. Equally erratic windows on the south side of the museum, by the ramp to the roof, spell out "CWM MCG" for Canadian War Museum and Musée Canadien de la Guerre.

Developed in the 1830s, Morse Code is a form of telecommunication that uses dots, dashes and spaces to represent the alphabet, numbers and punctuation. Codes are usually transmitted as electrical pulses or visual signals. "This would be different than a cipher or secret code," explains Dr. Tim Cook, the museum's chief historian and director of research. "Morse Code is just meant to convey crucial information over long distances." These messages are from lead architect Raymond Moriyama. "The museum almost seems to emerge from the landscape and goes from a lower point to a higher point, and it's the higher point that has the fin with the morse code on it," says Cook. "Architects don't always overtly come out and talk about all the features in their buildings," he adds.

Opened in 2005, the museum's stunning, purpose-built space in LeBreton Flats was designed by Toronto's Moriyama & Teshima Architects and Ottawa's Griffiths Rankin Cook Architects. The gently sloping roof boasts vegetation and copper sheathing, plus a rooftop Memorial Garden. On the eastern side, Moriyama Regeneration Hall is a dramatic vertical space designed as an architectural representation of the power of hope.

A triangular, floor-to-ceiling window offers a tightly framed view of the Peace Tower (see ch. 81). While the morse code windows are discussed on tours and by floor staff, there's strangely no actual signage about them.

Address 1 Vimy Place, Ottawa, ON K1A 0M8, +1 (819) 776-7000, www.warmuseum.ca |
Getting there O-Train to Pimisi (Line 1), then walk 10 minutes | Hours Wed, Fri–Sun
9am–4pm, Thu 9am–7pm | Tip The National Holocaust Monument reminds us to remain
vigilant "in standing guard against antisemitism, hatred and intolerance" (1918 Chaudière
Crossing, www.canada.ca).

71 Mother House Sundials

Ottawa's oldest public timepiece

Something unusual and not immediately identifiable is on two facing sides of a limestone building at Sussex Drive and Bruyère Street. It looks like two mismatched clocks, or abstract suns with light rays emanating from them. There are nine roman numerals on one façade and another nine, some the same, some different, on the other. So, it's not a traditional clock.

A plaque on the Mother House of the Sisters of Charity of Ottawa reveals that this sight is a vertical sundial. It was added in 1851 by Father Jean-François Allard from France. He was a spiritual advisor to the nuns who lived here, but also a geography, geometry and math professor with a passion for science.

The unassuming, often-overlooked sundial, one of several across the city, is Ottawa's first public timepiece and the second oldest in North America. It maintains the correct time. "A sundial is a device where time is marked by the shadow of a rod (gnomon)," reads a Mother House brochure. "This means that the measurement of time is based on the apparent position of the sun." The dials are made of gray plaster with black, painted iron gnomons to show the time by the position of its shadow with Roman numerals. The southeast sundial facing Bruyère "declines in the morning because it is illuminated by the sun at this time of day. The hour-lines VII to III mark the time from sunrise until noon," the brochure explains. The southwest sundial facing Sussex declines in the afternoon. The hour-lines X to VII mark the time from noon to sunset.

Sister Élisabeth Bruyère helped the Sisters of Charity, also known as the Grey Nuns of the Cross, take up residence here in 1845 "to care for the poor and the sick and to educate the young." The convent grew into Ottawa's first hospital and is now beside the Élisabeth Bruyère Hospital. The charming sundials, says Superior General Rachelle Watier, "are part of our legacy."

Address 9 Bruyère Street, Ottawa, ON K1N 5C9, +1 (613) 241-2710, www.soeursdelachariteottawa.com | Getting there O-Train to Rideau (Line 1) | Hours Unrestricted | Tip In front of the David Ewart-designed Dominion Observatory building is a large floral sundial. Gravel and flower beds form the dial's face between the hour lines (1 Observatory Crescent).

72 National Gallery Stairs
Climb to new heights

People come to the National Gallery of Canada for the art, but not many take time to appreciate the architecture, especially the stairs. Staff nicknamed them the "elephant stairs," as elephants could theoretically carry royalty up them. The iconic 1988 building, a light-splashed structure of glass and granite, was designed by Montreal architect Moshe Safdie. You come into the L-shaped gallery through the entry pavilion to the Great Hall, then turn right towards the Ottawa River to go down a long hallway to the library, cafeteria, contemporary galleries and curatorial wing.

While you won't find anything written about the stairs' backstory, there is an illuminating 2010 video interview with Safdie on the National Gallery's YouTube channel. "So, this L shape meant that while you've got the great ramp open to the city, leading you up to the Great Hall, once you make that right turn, you're embedded by galleries on both sides, and it's an interior space," says Safdie in the video. "And I thought it should have a sense of ceremony and be monumental enough to draw you in. It's like coming more into, I wouldn't call it the tomb, but at least into the sort of innards of the building."

Safdie had just visited Egypt and was taken with "the scale of the great ramp walkways, particularly at Karnak." He thought people could move horizontally through the National Gallery hallway, but to access the upper level or library, they could ascend via "a sort of step ramp as they would in Egypt or in Rome, and give it a kind of an almost archaeological sense." This concourse is flat on one side with a ramp on the other that leads up to the rotunda or what Safdie calls "the octagon."

The National Gallery, established in 1880 with just one 19th-century landscape painting, now holds more than 75,000 works of art and one of the world's best Indigenous and Canadian art collections.

Address 380 Sussex Drive, Ottawa, ON K1N 9N4, +1 (613) 990-1985, www.gallery.ca, info@gallery.ca | Getting there O-Train to Rideau (Line 1) | Hours Wed, Fri–Sun 10am–5pm, Thu 10am–8pm | Tip The Canada Council for the Arts' Âjagemô art space, open weekdays with free admission, hosts contemporary Canadian art exhibitions, events and performances (150 Elgin Street, www.canadacouncil.ca).

73 Oat Couture

Mecca for oatmeal aficionados

Oat Couture claims to be the only oatmeal café chain in Canada and possibly the world. Come here to try "fashionable oatmeal." The two-branch café uses steel-cut oats from Saskatchewan – hulled and toasted whole-grain groat, that are chopped into smaller bits. The result is chewier and nuttier than instant or flaked oatmeal options. And at Oat Culture, the naturally gluten-free oats are cooked in Instant Pots with water and a little salt. Try stirring in some Oatgurt, an oat milk-based yogurt.

You can customize bowls or pick from 18 in-house creations. Sweet options include Lunchbox (banana, almond butter, dates, coconut, raspberry purée) and Sorrento (blueberry compote, toasted almonds, lemon curd). Savoury choices range from Hangover (cheddar, apple, bacon, lemon juice, caramelized onion, thyme and maple syrup) and Caprese (sundried tomato, goat cheese, prosciutto, basil and caper pesto). There's granola, overnight oats, paninis on oat ciabattas, and breakfast sandwiches with oat hollandaise sauce.

All the baked goods have an oat twist, and seasonal smoothies are made with oats and oat milk. "It's such a heart-healthy grain, and it's so good for you," says café owner Brian Montgomery, who is also a portfolio manager and investment adviser. "You can do anything you would do with risotto or quinoa. It's whatever you stir in and whatever toppings you choose."

The original, highly Instagrammable café launched on Bank Street in Old Ottawa South in 2018, and a second, larger location in Centretown West opened in 2021 on Gladstone Avenue. Both are staffed almost exclusively with students and give back to the community. The OC Breakfast Club hands out about a dozen meal bags daily, each with an oatmeal bowl, from a cart out front. In another twist, both spots transform into the Montgomery Scotch Lounge at night to feature single malt scotches and scotch cocktails.

Address 1154 Bank Street, Ottawa, ON K1S 3X6, +1 (613) 737-6654, www.oatcouturecafe.com, teamoatmeal@oatcouturecafe.com | Getting there Bus 7 to Bank/ Belmont | Hours Daily 7am–5pm | Tip Nearby is a bronze statue of the late Sri Chinmoy, the controversial Indian spiritual leader who promoted meditation and athleticism (northeast corner of Bank Street and Belmont Avenue).

74 Ottawa Aviation Adventures

Soar in the open cockpit of a vintage plane

Ottawa's only airplane sightseeing company will take you back in time and up into the skies in its vintage 1939 and 1940 biplanes. "It's a completely different flying experience for most people," says Ottawa Aviation Adventures owner Greg Reynolds. "It's very immersive, open cockpit, wind through the hair. If you pick a nice, sunny day, it's like flying around in a convertible car over downtown Ottawa." With everyone wearing leather helmets and goggles, it's also reminiscent of *The English Patient*, the 1996 romantic war drama that featured biplanes. You can borrow scarves after the flight for photos, but you can't wear them during the flight since they can blow back into the pilot's face.

Reynolds fell for aviation when he was six years old. His dad loved operating radio-controlled airplanes as a hobby, and he followed suit by learning to build them. After flight management school at Confederation College, he flew float planes into remote fishing and hunting camps, and then he flew with various airlines in the arctic before pursuing his passion for vintage aircraft. Reynolds launched this company in 1995 with one biplane and now has two, plus a Cessna 172 to run family flights. The company is based at Rockcliffe Airport, with a ticket counter inside the Canada Aviation and Space Museum (see ch. 100). Reynolds serves as chief pilot for the biplanes and has several other pilots that help with the biplanes and family flights.

Biplane tours hold two passengers and start at 10 to 15 minutes for views of Parliament Hill and downtown, or lower altitude flights over the Ottawa River. There are slightly longer options to fly over Quebec's Gatineau River or as far as the Champlain Lookout in Gatineau Park. Sunset flights are popular. The Cessna holds three passengers for family tours that fly similar routes. Ride with Santa during pre-Christmas fundraising flights.

Address 1495 Sir George-Étienne Cartier Parkway, Ottawa, ON K1K 4Y5, +1 (613) 315-7229, www.ottawaaviationadventures.com, ottawabiplane@gmail.com | Getting there Bus 25 to Aviation Museum | Hours Biplanes: daily 8am–6pm May 1–Oct 31, family flights year-round | Tip Take a tour of or a ride in Vintage Wings of Canada's restored and working aircraft by reservation at Gatineau-Ottawa Executive Airport (1699 Rue Arthur Fecteau, Gatineau, www.vintagewings.ca).

75   Ottawa Bike Café
Pitstop for the cycle fiends

When Maria Rasouli was growing up in a village in northern Iran, she adored exploring the fields and forest by bike with her best friend perched on the handlebars. "As a kid, I was so free and so happy," she remembers. But when she was almost 12, her parents announced that cycling was no longer an appropriate pastime for a woman, and she had to pass the beloved bike on to her brother.

Thirteen years later, Rasouli came to Carleton University to pursue her PhD in organizational psychology and made sure she had a place to live – and a bike waiting for her. Taking it for a spin was the first thing Rasouli did after taking a taxi to her rental and dropping her luggage. The feelings of "freedom and joy" returned instantly, and she quickly came to appreciate what the city offers to cyclists. "Where I grew up, there were no bike paths. This is a heaven, a source of inspiration, with 600 kilometres to ride."

Rasouli did an unsatisfying few years of office work before striking out as the owner of Escape Bicycle Tours and Rentals in 2015, and co-owner of the Ottawa Bike Café in 2021. The seasonal tour/rental company (open from April to November) lets her combine her love of biking with her love of Ottawa. The café is a place where everyone who loves bikes can gather to eat good food, have a beer or just enjoy an ice cream. Rasouli's café partner is Jason Komendat, owner of Retro-Rides, a bike shop that looks at "each bicycle as a rolling piece of functional art." All three businesses are housed under the same Sparks Street roof.

The café has a 40-seat patio and sells hot and cold beverages. The coffee menu includes almost any drink you want, from espressos and cappuccinos to turmeric and dirty chai lattes. E-Berry, an elderberry hibiscus tea, is popular, as are the baked goods, ice cream, peanut butter toast, grilled cheese, soups, roasted nuts and popcorn. Coffee beans are proudly sourced from Fluid, an off-grid company that solar roasts an hour away.

Retro-Rides.ca

& SERVICE

Address 79 Sparks Street, Ottawa, ON K1P 5A5, +1 (343) 996-9487, www.bikecafe.ca, ottawabikecafe@gmail.com | Getting there O-Train to Parliament (Line 1) | Hours Mon–Fri 8am–5pm, Sat & Sun 10am–5pm | Tip Apothecary Lounge serves drinks from the Swalwell-Borbridge Building that dates back to 1875, while "paying homage to our bootlegging ancestors" (54 York Street, www.apothecarylounge.ca).

76__Ottawa Little Theatre

Always say goodnight to Martha

Her name is Martha, and she's the Ottawa Little Theatre's beloved resident ghost, a benevolent spirit that has long been behind perplexing noises, strange lights and moving shapes. The Eastern Methodist Church once stood here, reportedly with an unconsecrated graveyard. The community theatre company bought the decommissioned property and renovated it into a theatre that opened in 1928. Things were quiet until the building was destroyed by a 1970 electrical fire, and the theatre was forced to rebuild.

It was at this time, between 1970 and 1972, that a stone (possibly a gravestone) bearing the name Martha was reportedly uncovered during excavating for a parking lot to expand the building's footprint. The stone was unfortunately discarded, but the name Martha stuck. And the mysterious encounters began.

People – usually long-time volunteers – are more likely to hear or feel Martha than to see her, often on play nights after the crowd has left. Board President Geoff Gruson says the last person leaving always shouts, "Goodnight, Martha!" Once, when he was crossing the stage to exit and hadn't yet said farewell, he felt a tingling, turned and looked up at the two catwalks. "In the darkness, I saw this glimmering, sort of shimmering, grey-white shape of a woman in a long gown." The not-for-profit theatre has produced more than 1,000 plays since it launched in 1913 as the Ottawa Drama League. It is Canada's – and maybe North America's – oldest, still-running community theatre company, and it aims to put "a little theatre in everyone's life." It usually produces a nine-play season, drawing upwards of 50,000 patrons to its 386-seat auditorium each year.

Martha is mentioned in *Love and Whisky: The Story of the Dominion Drama Festival and the Early Years of Theatre in Canada 1606–1972* by Betty Lee and *Staging a Legend: A History of Ottawa Little Theatre* by Iris Winston.

Address 400 King Edward Avenue, Ottawa, ON K1N 7M7, +1 (613) 233-8948, www.ottawalittletheatre.com, foh@ottawalittletheatre.com | Getting there O-Train to Rideau (Line 1) | Hours See website for schedule and showtimes | Tip The 1830s-era Rochon Residence, one of the city's original timber homes, has been restored for an artist-in-residence program to reanimate federal heritage buildings (138 St. Patrick Street, www.ncc-ccn.gc.ca).

77 Ottawa Public Library

Attention Brutalism lovers

It's one of the city's last remaining Brutalist gems, and its future is uncertain. The main branch of the Ottawa Public Library dates to 1974. It was built at the end of a post-war building boom from the 1950s to 1970s, when an extensive use of concrete and minimal use of windows countered the early 20th-century years of modernist glass and steel buildings. Designed by prolific Canadian architect George Bemi to replace the deteriorating 1906 Carnegie Library, the controversial library with the striking white, precast concrete façade soon won the Award of Merit from the Royal Architectural Institute of Canada but was later named one of the city's ugliest buildings by the *Ottawa Citizen* in 2014.

"The architect distances the building from its curtain wall dominated surroundings by rendering the entire façade in exposed concrete," explains #SOSBrutalism, a global online database of Brutalist buildings and "a platform for a large campaign to save our beloved concrete monsters." Sarah B. Gelbard, "part punk planner, part anarchitect" and co-director of yowLAB, an architecture and design ideas lab and community network, has led Brutalism talks and tours and believes the much-maligned architectural style should be cherished and protected. In a story for *Spacing Ottawa*, she likens Brutalist architecture to a blind date who has a great personality and the kind of unexpected beauty that comes from character.

Brutalist buildings are always at risk of being demolished and replaced. The more famously Brutalist National Arts Centre has been filled with light in a recent revamp. The central library is slated to move to spectacular new digs in LeBreton Flats in 2024 or 2025 and share space with Library and Archives Canada. There's no word on the fate of the Metcalfe Street building or its stained-glass window from the Carnegie era that honours literature and famous authors.

Address 120 Metcalfe Street, Ottawa, ON K1P 5M2, +1 (613) 580-2940, www.biblioottawalibrary.ca | Getting there O-Train to Parliament (Line 1) | Hours Exterior is unrestricted; see website for library hours | Tip Ottawa's last library financed by Andrew Carnegie is the Rosemount Branch, with wood shelving, arched windows and high ceilings (18 Rosemount Avenue, www.biblioottawalibrary.ca).

78 Ottawa Tool Library
Lending tools instead of books

Proudly part of the sharing economy, the Ottawa Tool Library (OTL) loans hand-, power-, kitchen and gardening tools to people working on DIY projects. The thinking is that modern-day urbanites don't stockpile these tools like previous generations did. People don't have room or don't want to buy them for just one project. Bettina Vollmerhausen, co-founder, executive director and tool goddess, started the non-profit library in 2015. The OTL grew out of its first small location and moved to this new location in 2021. There is now room for more than 2,500 tools that can be borrowed for up to a week by anyone who's at least 18 years old. Check out axes, bandsaws, belt sanders, brick chisels, convection countertop ovens, ice cream makers, grass trimmers and hand pruners, to name just a few.

Beyond reaping the obvious environmental, community and cost benefits, Ottawa's first tool library aims to help people access tools and learn how to use them. There is a workspace and room for workshops, demo nights and repair cafés. The library hosts classes on everything from knife sharpening and plumbing to tile setting, bike repair and rustic furniture building. As Vollmerhausen puts it, "The goal is for people to lose that fear of tools and become comfortable."

More than 2,000 people have joined with monthly or annual memberships since the OTL started, and there are usually several hundred active members. Workshops are open to everyone. The volunteer-driven organization relies on tool donations, and there's a "tool wish list" on its website. "Tool doctors" triage the donations at the Dr. Phil Yang Memorial Tool Hospital, named for the first tool doctor, assessing the library's needs and determining which tools to donate to community gardens or other non-profits. Some donations are sold through the library's web store, which evolved from the popular annual garage sales.

Address 877A Boyd Avenue, Ottawa, ON K2A 2E2, +1 (613) 868-0178 (entrance off Dobbie Street), www.ottawatoollibrary.com, info@ottawatoollibrary.com | Getting there Bus 50 to Clyde North / Lapierre | Hours Tue – Fri 5 – 8pm, Sat 10am – 1pm | Tip The Ottawa Outdoor Gear Library believes in "just access to nature-based experiences for all" and gives members unlimited access to outdoor equipment for five days (877A Boyd Avenue, www.ottawaoutdoorgearlibrary.com).

79— Parliament Hill Stairs

A steep and scenic shortcut

They zig and zag about a dozen times from the top of the steep escarpment behind the Parliament Buildings down to the shore of the Ottawa River. Runners and joggers gravitate to them. Others find the Parliament Hill Escarpment Stairway serendipitously and fall in love. The escarpment was once a healthy forest full of white pines, oaks, sugar maples, beech and hemlocks, but invasive plants with large canopies took over, the soil eroded and the ground became unstable. The government is working hard to restore the area to its "natural forested state."

The stairway connecting the Hill with the river is the first landscape intervention on Parliament Hill in 100 years. Designed to meet heritage conservation standards, the modern stairway helps people "stroll" through a rugged forest while enjoying stunning river views. It's the work of the Ottawa team of the Civitas Group, who won a 2018 National Award for Small-Scale Public Landscapes Designed by a Landscape Architect (up to one hectare or 2.5 acres) from the Canadian Society of Landscape Architects for the project.

To find the stairway, walk along the west side of the main Parliament Building, past the House of Commons visitor entrance and various statues towards the escarpment. Watch for the retro signs on the pathway at the bottom of the stairs, some of which just warn against poison ivy. The grounds of Parliament Hill, originally designed by landscape architect Calvert Vaux, are a Classified heritage landscape, and they are as important as the buildings. As you explore this national landmark, you'll notice the wonderful contrast between the jagged escarpment and the elegant lawns and structures.

The invasive species have prevented the native vegetation from flourishing on the escarpment, but work is quietly underway to stabilize the slopes and diversify the plant life, which should in turn allow for more varied fall colours.

Address 111 Wellington Street, Ottawa, ON K1A 0A6, +1 (613) 992-4793, https://visit.parl.ca, info@parl.gc.ca | Getting there O-Train to Parliament (Line 1) | Hours Unrestricted | Tip Every year from May to August, there's free yoga sponsored by Lululemon on Wednesdays at noon, weather permitting, on the Parliament Hill lawn (111 Wellington Street, www.ottawatourism.ca/en/see-and-do/yoga-parliament-hill).

80 Patinage en Forêt

Skate through an enchanting forest

When Dave Mayer saw a YouTube video in January 2016 about a skating trail through a pine forest in northern Quebec, he knew instantly that it was something he and wife Monique Robert must do with their property at the edge of Gatineau Park. They had the forest with spruce, balsam, birch and only the odd red pine on 100 acres that's been in his family since the early 1800s. They had the skills, since he's a general contractor who builds homes and cottages. By December, they had cut a three-kilometre (1.8-mile) trail, flooded it and created Patinage en Forêt (Skating Through the Forest). He modestly hoped to get 3,000 people that first season. They hosted 3,000 per week.

"We say it's magical here because people tell us all the time that we create happiness," says Mayer. People come from around the world for the experience, which he keeps as pristine as possible by not having any music or artificial lights. Food and drinks include soup, chili, hot dogs, cocoa, coffee, pop and wolf's tails, a spin on BeaverTails (see ch. 12). There are no deep fryers to interfere with the fresh, country air. Almost everybody skates during the daylight, and on Fridays, 400 kerosene lights are set out for "torchlight evenings."

The one-way skating trail is three metres (10 feet) wide and horseshoe shaped. It has a couple of cross trails for shortcuts, about 50 benches and multiple leaning posts. There's 10,000 square metres (12,000 square yards) of ice, which Mayer's team does its best to keep in impeccable shape. Weather permitting, the season starts around December 20th and runs through the first week of March. Also enjoy a walking trail for a stroll and a snowshoe trail, both three kilometres (1.8 miles) long.

There's even a crokicurl rink (a mashup of crokinole and curling). The quintessentially Canadian skating experience is near the village of Lac-des-Loups (Wolf Lake).

Address 9 Montée Beausoleil, Lac-des-Loups, ON QC J0X 3K0, +1 (819) 456-1444, www.patinageenforet.com, aucoueurdulacdesloups@gmail.com | Getting there By car, Autoroute 5 to Quebec Route 366, then follow signs to destination | Hours Dec–Mar daily 9am–dusk, weather permitting | Tip Year-round adventure park Arbraska Laflèche offers snowshoeing, winter ziplining, cave exploration, hikes and more (255 Route Principale, Val-des-Monts, https://en.arbraska.com/park/lafleche).

81 Peace Tower Flag
Join the city's longest waiting list

"Dear Madam: This is to acknowledge receipt of your request for a flag that has flown from Parliament Hill in Ottawa. We confirm that the requested name has been added to the waiting list. The waiting period for both Peace Tower and other Parliament Hill flags exceeds 100 years." Beyond just admiring the Canadian flag that flies from the 98-metre-high Peace Tower, you can go online and request one. They are free with three catches: you must be Canadian, there's only one request per household and the waiting list is longer than most people's lives. And yet, why not dream about getting one of the 250-odd flags a year that are flown?

Canada used the Union Jack and Canadian Red Ensign before creating its own flag. In 1964, under Prime Minister Lester B. Pearson, three designs were shortlisted. Civil servant Ken Donovan enlisted his daughter Joan O'Malley to make the prototypes – her sewing machine is at the Canadian Museum of History (see ch. 45). A red-and-white design by George Stanley with a single red maple leaf, already a symbol of Canadian identity, was chosen. Stanley was a former army lieutenant-colonel, military historian and dean of arts at the Royal Military College, whose design was inspired by the college's flag. The new flag was first raised on the Hill on February 15, 1965.

Now a flag master changes the 2.3-metre by 4.6-metre Peace Tower flag every weekday (except on statutory holidays and during poor weather) and on half-masting occasions. The other four Parliament Hill flags – over the West Block, East Block and each side of the Centre Block – are changed weekly and on half-mast days. The flag master folds a Peace Tower flag, puts it in a satchel, rides the elevator to the observation deck, climbs 33 metres of stairs and ladders, lowers the flying flag and raises the new one. It takes 20 to 30 minutes and the flag isn't allowed to touch the ground.

Address 111 Wellington Street, Ottawa, ON K1A 0A6, +1 (613) 992-4793, https://visit.parl.ca, info@parl.gc.ca | **Getting there** O-Train to Parliament (Line 1) | **Hours** Unrestricted from the outside | **Tip** On April 3, 1957, Elvis was in the house, or rather the Senate. He arrived at Ottawa's original central train station, which was temporarily housing the Senate of Canada and was whisked away in a limo (2 Rideau Street, www.sencanada.ca).

82 — Petrie Island Turtles
Protecting aquatic creatures

If you're strolling along Turtle Trail in the summer, watch for thigh-high mesh towers wrapped around wooden spikes on sandy patches of land. These are turtle nests that are being protected from hungry predators. For $2, you can sponsor a protected egg as part of the ongoing turtle conservation efforts by Friends of Petrie Island.

The Petrie Island group, with about 12 kilometres (7.5 miles) of shoreline, are on the Ottawa River. They were formed by sand deposited at the end of the last ice age, about 12,000 years ago. The Friends of Petrie Island formed in 1988 to help conserve the western portion of the islands and the development of passive recreation facilities for future generations to appreciate this natural treasure.

Petrie Island likes to call itself "a small wilderness." It's also a park made up of conservation areas and picnic spots managed by volunteers, and North / River and East Bay public beaches run by the City of Ottawa. Sunbathers, picnickers, paddlers, boaters, birders, anglers, hikers, volleyball players and nature lovers all gravitate here. Ottawa Marina East at Petrie Island rents canoes and kayaks, and its winter ice fishing packages come complete with ice huts and gear.

Mind the poison ivy, pay for parking and do spend some time with the turtles. Named for the colourful markings on their shells and bellies, northern painted turtles are one of Petrie's most visible and beloved aquatic residents. They hang out in ponds, lakes and streams and lurk among lily pads and pickerel weed. In winter, these cold-blooded reptiles live under the mud at the bottom of the ponds. From late spring to mid-summer, the females find sandy spots to dig nests and lay eggs, and then hatchlings try to evade gulls, crows, raccoons and dogs. The short Turtle Trail follows a pond, where you might also see snapping turtles or map turtles basking in the sun or researchers catching turtles to mark, weigh and release.

Address Petrie Islands, accessed by Trim Road, Orléans, ON, www.petrieisland.org, inquiries@petrieisland.org | Getting there Bus 38 to Inlet/Trim, then walk 17 minutes | Hours Daily 6am–9pm | Tip Drive through Parc Oméga to see Canadian animals, including elk, bison, moose and bears. Stay overnight to be surrounded by a pack of grey wolves (399 Quebec 323 N, Montebello, www.parcomega.ca).

83 Pimisi Station's Eel

O-Train honours Algonquin culture

In the Algonquin language, *pimisi* means "eel." The snake-like fish has a sacred significance and has been a source of spirituality, medicine and food for thousands of years. Eels have long been part of the traditional Algonquin economy and were often smoked so they could be eaten throughout winter.

Pimisi is also the name of the first light rail station west of downtown on the Confederation line, under the Booth Street Bridge. Designed to reflect the historical and contemporary significance of the Algonquin people, the station has an upper street level, an intermediate platform level and a lower concourse and public plaza with free access.

It's in this plaza that you will find Algonquin artist Nadia Myre's untitled *pimisi/e*el sculpture in the centre of a heritage aqueduct. The eight-metre (26-foot) chromed eel is "a beacon and a landmark" for the station. It stands vertically with its head diving into a fissure between rocks, as its surface reflects and disappears into the surroundings. Myre, a visual artist from Montreal, also created a split-ash basket made of interwoven steel bands and a birch forest fence (designs on glass platform walls) for an untitled 2018 trilogy that the city says is to "both celebrate Algonquin culture and to remind visitors of the fragile ecosystem that we inhabit."

American eels once thrived in the Ottawa River but have been nearly decimated by harvesting and habitat contamination and destruction. Dams and turbines at hydroelectric generation stations block migration. A short walk away, at Chaudière Falls Powerhouse (see ch. 26), Portage Power has installed an eel ladder on the upstream side and two bypass channels on the downstream side for safe passage. For O-Train's Public Art Program, the Algonquin-themed Pimisi station only features artwork by Algonquin artists who collaborated with nearby Algonquin Anishinaabe communities.

Address South end of Booth Street Bridge, Ottawa, ON K1R 7V9, www.octranspo.com, +1 (613) 560-5000 | Getting there O-Train to Pimisi (Line 1) | Hours Plaza is unrestricted | Tip Explore LeBreton Flats on the universally accessible, one-kilometre (.6-mile), walk/bike path connecting the Capital Pathway along the Ottawa River to the Pimisi and Bayview O-Train stations (www.ncc-ccn.gc.ca).

84 Pinhey Sand Dunes
This forest has a secret beach but no water

It's an unusual sight in a capital city, one you'd rather expect alongside the ocean in a province like Prince Edward Island. The Pinhey Sand Dunes are a unique, inland ecosystem west of the airport. You can park near the corner of Pineland Avenue and Vaan Drive in Merivale Gardens, and an accessible portion of these unusual dunes with fine white sand is steps away.

A trail sign explains that this is the Pinhey Forest Sector, named for the man who donated the land for conservation, of Canada's Capital Greenbelt. A series of ropes and wires keep you away from restoration areas so the National Capital Commission can protect and maintain the sand dunes' environment. Still, there's lots of space to wander the open, sandy space between the trees and into the forest. Picnickers are welcome, and feel free to wander barefoot. Trail 32 offers a three-kilometre (1.8-mile) hike through two other areas of dunes.

This area was once the Champlain Sea, which dates back 10,000 years to the last glacial period. Southwesterly winds picked up sand from the exposed sea floor, deposited it here and then helped form it into dunes. Some hardy plants, insects and animals have adapted to the hot, sunny and exposed area, where extreme summer temperatures can climb to 72°C (162°F), and the sand is three- to five-feet deep.

Sadly, only a small percentage of the original dunes remain. Biodiversity Conservancy International started restoring and protecting the fragile dunes in 2012 so they wouldn't be wiped out. Stephen Aitken, coordinator of the Pinhey Sand Dunes Project, reports that trees and organic matter were removed, dirty sand was cleaned and dune plants were repopulated. Things are looking good for the ghost tiger beetle, which is nearly invisible and locally threatened, as well as the carnivorous antlion and the intriguing star fungus. You'll find occasional explanatory signs.

Address Slack Road, Ottawa, ON K2G, www.capitalgems.ca/pinhey-sand-dune-complex.html, contact@capitalgems.ca | Getting there Bus 187, 670 to Vaan / Slack | Hours Unrestricted | Tip Pick your own strawberries and raspberries every summer or get fresh produce, pies and jams at the Shouldice Berry Farm & Market (various locations, www.shouldicefarm.com).

85 __ Pink Lake
It isn't actually pink, but it is special

Pink Lake is actually very green. Named for the Pink family that settled the land in 1826, this a rare meromictic lake because the waters at the surface don't mix with the waters at the bottom like most lakes do every spring and fall. It's sheltered by cliffs that protect it from the winds that would trigger mixing.

From a depth of 13 metres (43 feet) to the bottom at 20 metres (66 feet), the water hasn't been in contact with air for more than 10,000 years. It contains no oxygen. But just below the 13-metre mark is a dense pink cloud of sulphur-bacteria, one of the first life forms. Below that is total darkness. Fish and animals must stay at the top of the lake to survive.

Most people come to see Pink Lake during the summer, when the water is a brilliant shade of green from large amounts of algae. Most of the surrounding rocks contain phosphate, a natural fertilizer, and as the rocks erode, it's washed into the lake, where it sparks the growth of microscopic algae. "Green water may be pleasing to the eye," reads one interpretation panel, "but it means that the lake is aging quickly and prematurely."

Nobody took much notice of this tiny green lake in Gatineau Park until the 1960s. Then a study showed that in spring, there is some algae from the previous year, but it's scarce and eaten by aquatic organisms. From June to August, the warm water speeds up algae growth, and the lake appears greener. In fall, that growth slows, and in winter the algae is dormant under the ice. This fragile area was once the Champlain Sea and transformed to freshwater very slowly over 3,000 years, giving the three-spined stickleback, an ocean fish, time to adapt and make its home in Pink Lake.

Pink Lake Lookout has sweeping views and interpretation panels. Pink Lake Trail is a 2.5-kilometre (1.5-mile) loop along pine walkways, stairs and three-season trails. Swimming is banned.

Address Pink Lake Lookout Parking Lot, Gatineau Park, QC, www.ncc-ccn.gc.ca, info@ncc-ccn.ca | Getting there By car, take Quebec Route 148 W to Boulevard Saint Raymond, turn left on Chemin Pink, right on Chemin de la Montagne North, right on Notch, then left on Gatineau Parkway to lookout or trail head. | Hours See website for seasonal hours and Gatineau Parkway restrictions | Tip Starting at Parent Beach Parking Lot at Lac Philippe, it's a 10-kilometre (6-mile) round-trip hike to Lusk Cave, created 12,500 years ago when the Wisconsin Glacier melted (300 Chemin du Lac-Philippe, Sainte-Cécile-de-Masham, www.ncc-ccn.gc.ca/places/lusk-cave).

86 Poets' Pathway

Get outside to honour Confederation poets

By the edge of the Ottawa River in Britannia Park is a bronze plaque affixed to a rock, marking the first of a dozen sections on the Poets' Pathway. The plaque includes 15 lines from *The Song My Paddle Sings* by Emily Pauline Johnson (1861–1913).

Born on the Six Nations Reserve in what is now Ontario to a Mohawk chief father and English immigrant mother, Johnson adopted the name Tekahionwake ("Double Wampum"). Instead of marrying and having children as was the norm, she created Mohawk and Victorian costumes and toured the country as a performer. She is lauded as one of the first Indigenous poets published in Canada and one of the few female writers / performers from that era who made a living from her art.

The Poet's Pathway honours Canada's poets (especially those from Ottawa, like Archibald Lampman and Charles Sangster), who came to prominence after Confederation in 1867, and the land that inspired them. As Johnson's plaque explains, *[The pathway] memorializes the literary heritage of the Confederation Poets and francophone poets of the time, the earliest voices of our distinctive Canadian traditions.*

Calling the 19th-century Confederation poets "the literary equivalent of the Group of Seven," the volunteer founders of this pathway-in-progress have been creating a walking / biking trail that criss-crosses about 35 kilometres (22 miles) of existing trails from Britannia Beach in the West to Poet's Hill in Beechwood Cemetery, the resting place of five of Ottawa's major Confederation poets, in the East. Poem snippets are engraved on plaques in natural settings.

Britannia Park is one of three anchors for the pathway, and selecting Johnson's work for the first plaque acknowledges that Indigenous people travelled and lived along the river for centuries. Find the plaque west of the park's main beach, past the G. B. Greene anchor and in between some of the rocky piers.

Address Britannia Park, Ottawa, ON K2B 6Z9, www.poetspathway.ca, info@poetspathway.ca |
Getting there Bus 51 to Britannia/Selina | Hours Unrestricted | Tip Make an advance
booking to visit the Library and Archives Canada, with 20-million books, 30-million
photographic images, and 425,000 works of art (395 Wellington Street, www.bac-lac.gc.ca).

87 Railbender Tattoo Studio

Hintonburg tattoo parlour's spirit animal

For tattoo artist Julien Detillieux, cats are an important recurring theme in both his work and personal life. He and his girlfriend Melissa have been fostering cats for years, and while he specializes in colourful neotraditional work often blended with realism, he also loves to do cat-related pieces. He has a cat drinking bubble tea tattooed on his own leg. As Detillieux tells the story, when "anime nerd" Serena Armstrong joined Railbender Tattoo Studio, she was constantly ordering bubble tea and introduced him to it. It's also common for artists to "trade" tattoos, and when Armstrong agreed to give him one, he gave her free reign to design it. She said it would "obviously be a cat," and he asked if bubble tea could be incorporated.

And the cat connection goes deeper. When he was first trying to find an apprenticeship, Detillieux checked out Railbender, but nothing came of it. Then the founder, Alex Néron, and his wife, Marta Jarzabek, applied to the Ottawa Stray Cat Rescue. Detillieux happened to be assigned to interview them for an adoption, something his girlfriend usually did. They were approved. Later, Detillieux went to Railbender for a tattoo, and realizing the cat connection, he landed the coveted apprenticeship in 2016 and started working his way up. Sadly, Néron died of cancer in 2018, and Detillieux bought the business in 2020 – just before COVID hit.

Railbender is named as a homage to the Hintonburg neighbourhood's railroad history. It started out doubling as an art gallery, with exhibitions by local artists and sometimes international artists with local roots. But to make ends meet after multiple COVID closures, Detillieux converted the gallery into a space for a third tattoo artist. There's still art on the walls, though. And outside, a sprawling, colourful mural by Ottawa artist Arpi incorporates whales, birds and Néron's tattooed arm.

Address 3 Hamilton Avenue N, Ottawa, ON K1Y 1B4, +1 (613) 725-6061, www.railbenderstudio.com, info@railbenderstudio.com | Getting there O-Train to Tunney's Pasture (Line 1) | Hours By appointment | Tip The Foxhole Barber + Shop offers grooming services along with grooming products and curated sportswear, from denim to footwear (1206 Wellington Street W, www.thefoxholeshop.com).

88 Record Centre

Sell records, make records, celebrate music

Music lover and long-time collector John Thompson sells vinyl out of his Hintonburg shop, of course, but also vintage turntables, audio gear and speakers. He runs a custom record label for local artists and has hosted more than 500 in-store shows. He even nabbed a second space for his discount annex and processes requests for online sales from across North America. "I would not have done it if it wasn't right across the street," Thompson admits. "We have an inventory of 20,000 records on site and needed to be more organized. I also have five warehouses full of records."

Thompson grew up with vinyl and dabbled in CDs and cassettes. "I still enjoy the ritual and the sound of vinyl – it never left my house," he muses. "There's a cult around it, eh? Some people are super passionate about it."

He spent a decade selling vinyl and vintage audio on eBay before jumping into a shared bricks-and-mortar space in 2011. Three years later, when Character Hair Salon relinquished its space – with exposed brick walls and restored tin ceiling – he moved in. "We grew slowly, and that's probably part of our success," says Thompson.

He buys "well cared for record collections and quality vintage audio" and will even make house calls for larger collections. Genres of interest are rock, jazz, blues, Français, classical, country, bluegrass, punk, metal, reggae / ska, funk, soul, folk and spoken word. On the gear front, the shop covets vintage tables by Thorens, Dual, Technics, Garrard, Lenco and the like, as well as audio gear and speakers. There's a cozy listening section at the back.

Thompson launched his Record Centre Records label in 2015 and has released more than 48 albums by Juno Award-winning artists like MonkeyJunk and Paul Reddick, Oh Susanna and Steve Hill, as well as Telecomo, Heavy Medicine Band and Ian Tamblyn. The custom label usually presses 300 pieces.

Address 1099 Wellington Street W (main store) and 1112 Wellington Street W, Ottawa, ON K1Y 2Y4, +1 (613) 695-4577, www.therecordcentre.com | Getting there Bus 11 to Wellington / Carruthers | Hours Mon–Sat 10am–6pm, Sun noon–4pm | Tip In a former 1920s-era bread factory, the Enriched Bread Artists Studios host exhibitions, events and an open studio event every year in October (951 Gladstone Avenue, www.enrichedbreadartists.com).

89 Red Bird
Building a musical hub

Ottawa's first "live music centre" has three interwoven things going on. Red Bird is the brainchild of musician Geoff Cass from Gentlemen of the Woods. Launched in 2022 during the pandemic, it is a concert venue, a music school and café all in one space that started as an auto body shop. It boasts thick, concrete walls, floors and ceilings with no beams to obstruct sightlines, not to mention top-of-the-line sound and lights.

The venue seats about 80 people at high-top tables at the back and couches and armchairs at the front. "It's an amazing place for musicians to play," says Cass, "and for people to come and see a show." The intimate space books local bands and bigger touring acts looking to do sets in a smaller space. The plan is for opening acts at 8pm, headliners at 9pm and shows to end by a reasonable 11:30pm. They always host Bluegrass Mondays – a longstanding tradition in Ottawa.

There are five private teaching spaces and one group space for classes, workshops and lectures, all of which ties in with the fact Cass used to work for the Dovercourt Recreation Association and Bluesfest School of Music and Art. You can study banjo, bass, cello, drums, guitar, piano, song writing, theory, trumpet, ukulele and voice. A café gives people "a musical place to hang out" and play ukulele, guitar or piano while you're waiting for your significant other or kids to take lessons. The grab-and-go menu revolves around paninis, pizza and pastries.

And no, this isn't Canada's answer to the famed Bluebird Café in Nashville. Cass hasn't been and didn't make the connection when choosing the name. The red bird here is a cardinal drawn by Doug Taylor, a Gentlemen of the Woods bandmate, for the "alty folky, country, Americana-y" band's first album *Radiance*, and tweaked for the music venue. Look for the larger-than-life cardinal painted above the storefront on a rooftop wall.

Address 1165 Bank Street, Ottawa, ON K1S 3X7, www.redbirdlive.ca, info@redbirdlive.ca | Getting there Bus 6, 7 to Bank/Grove | Hours Mon–Fri 10:30am–9pm, Sat 10am–10pm, Sun 10am–5pm, see website for shows | Tip Gladstone Clayworks is a non-profit cooperative studio with a gallery and group classes in a former industrial bakery in Little Italy (949B Gladstone Avenue, www.gladstoneclayworks.ca).

90 — Remic Rapids Park Bunker
Oh, the things you can do with concrete

Remic Rapids Park hosts a mysterious oval bunker by a parking lot just down from the seasonal NCC Bistro. It's such a subtle structure that it blends right into the greenery along the rocky shore of the Ottawa River. But you are free to walk up a ramp to stand on the top of this concrete oddity and then meander around its rounded perimeter, as you search for meaning. Part of the mystery stems from the fact that there is no signage to say what the structure actually is. So, it's left to people's vivid imaginations. Capital Gems, a blog by local artist/author Andrew King, notes that people have mused over whether it might have been a nuclear reactor, a secret military bunker or a hydro station.

"The quirky bunker you see on the shoreline by Remic Rapids is actually part of a heating and cooling system that is connected to the Tunney's Pasture Campus," says Michèle LaRose, who handles media relations for Public Services and Procurement Canada, the government department that oversees the bunker. "A fascinating fact about this pumphouse is that the Government of Canada uses this bunker to pump river water to the Tunney's Pasture Energy Centre that provides heating and cooling to 16 buildings on the campus. This cuts the energy required to provide cooling to these buildings considerably which ultimately reduces our greenhouse gas emissions. The District Energy System itself is part of a larger multi-year modernization project."

Remic Rapids Park was once a popular trading and rest area for Indigenous people and early explorers. It's now the place to see John Felice Ceprano's ever-changing balanced rock sculptures and build your own along the shore. That bistro near the bunker? It has a patio that's perfect for sunsets. Order a hot dog, or veggie dog if you prefer, and a beer and settle in for vivid views of the river, Champlain Bridge and, of course, the bunker.

Address Sir John A. Macdonald Parkway, Ottawa, ON K1A 0K9, +1 (613) 239-5000, www.ncc-ccn.gc.ca/places/remic-rapids-park, info@ncc-ccn.ca | Getting there Bus 57, 61, 62, 63, 64 to Dominion 1a | Hours Daily 7am–10pm | Tip Raft trips down the Ottawa River with Ottawa City Rafting start at Britannia Beach, tackle the Deschenes Rapids and end with Parliament Hill views (102 Greenview Avenue, www.ottawacityrafting.com).

91 Rideau Canal Skateway

Test out Guinness-approved ice

Let's hear it directly from the folks at Guinness World Records: The Rideau Canal Skateway is officially the world's largest naturally frozen ice rink. It's 7.8 kilometres (4.8 miles) long and has a total maintained surface area of 165,621 square metres (1.782 million square feet) and the equivalent of 90 Olympic-sized skating rinks. "This is called an ice rink (as distinguished from any number of other frozen bodies of water) because its entire length received daily maintenance such as sweeping, ice thickness checks and there are toilet and recreational facilities along its entire length," reports www.guinessworldrecords.com.

In 1970–1971, National Capital Commission (NCC) chair Douglas Fullerton sent a crew with hand shovels to clear the first five kilometres between the National Arts Centre and the Bronson Avenue overpass for a giant skateway. The Skateway now runs from downtown along Colonel By Drive to Hartwells Locks. As the NCC puts it, Ottawa now has a skating surface that equals almost 140 National Hockey League rinks.

The iconic Skateway typically welcomes skaters from around the world beginning in January, through February's Winterlude festival and into March. The average skating season is 44 days, and recent seasons logged almost 1.5 million visits. Those Christmas trees decorating rest areas are either unsold trees recovered from merchants, or donations from people's homes after the holidays, and they're chipped and composted at the end of the season.

Be on the lookout for two kinds of ice. Clear ice forms naturally, while white ice is created by flooding the snow that covers the surface of the existing ice. Around the 2.6-kilometre (1.6-mile) mark, go ahead and skate under a pretty footbridge into the often-overlooked Patterson Creek part of the skateway. If you skate all the way to Hartwells Locks, pose with the "KM 7.8" marker.

Address Rideau Canal between downtown and Hartwells Locks, Ottawa, ON,
+1 (613) 239-5000, www.ncc-ccn.gc.ca/places/rideau-canal-skateway, info@ncc-ccn.ca |
Getting there O-Train to Carleton (Line 1) | Hours Unrestricted | Tip Nordik Spa-Nature is
all about thermotherapy and a hot-cold-rest ritual that takes you from saunas to cold pools to
relaxation areas (16 Chemin Nordik, Chelsea, https://chelsea.lenordik.com/en).

92 Rideau Hall's Sentries

Ceremonial duties with iconic bearskin hats

Rideau Hall has been the official residence and workplace of every governor general since 1867 and the only official residence in Ottawa that's open to the public. Forget Parliament Hill – this is the best place to see sentries in full-dress uniform each summer, with bearskin hats and scarlet tunics. The iconic hats were first adopted by the United Kingdom Grenadier Guards after the Battle of Waterloo in 1815 and then adopted by all Guard Regiments in 1831.

The caps are made from Canadian bear fur sourced at auctions across the country, according to Second Lieutenant Colin Schlachta, public affairs officer for the 33 Canadian Brigade Group of the Canadian Armed Forces. The chin straps are made of leather and brass, and the red plumes signify an assignment to the Governor General's Foot Guards, which was formed June 7, 1872. The caps are lovingly maintained and refurbished, but new ones are ordered in small batches as needed. "Soldiers' bearskins are about a foot tall, while officers' bearskins are 1.5 feet tall," reports Schlachta. "While being surprisingly light, (it) is extremely hot for the soldiers who don them during the summer months." When not in use, the prized caps are kept away from direct sunlight and stored in a temperature- and humidity-controlled environment. "For cleaning," says Schlachta, "like for human hair, the bearskin requires frequent brushing with applications of water."

The Ceremonial Guard is made up of trained members of regular and reserve forces. They do foot and rifle drills, music rehearsals and inspections. At 9am, a posting corporal marches out with four sentries, two escorts and a bagpiper. They march to the Sussex Drive gate of Rideau Hall, where two sentries are posted and read their duties. Then they march up to Rideau Hall itself to post the other two sentries. The sentries are relieved every hour on the hour until 5pm.

Address 1 Sussex Drive, Ottawa, ON K1A 0A1, +1 (613) 991-4422, www.gg.ca, guide@gg.ca | Getting there Bus 9 to Crichton/Dufferin, then walk 10 minutes | Hours Daily 8am–one hour before sunset | Tip The Governor General's Foot Guards Regimental Museum in the Cartier Square Drill Hall is run by volunteer curators and usually open Tuesday nights 7–9pm from September to May (2 Queen Elizabeth Drive, https://footguards.ca).

93　Riviera

Autograph from a bank robber

Today it's the Riviera, a fine dining restaurant with art deco flourishes and soaring ceilings. It serves Fogo Island cod, lobster spaghetti and a popular dish of mushrooms on toast with shaved black truffles. But in 1958, this was the Imperial Bank of Canada. And Boyne Lester Johnston, a married bank teller from Renfrew, walked out on October 26 with about $260,000 (more than $2.2 million today), fled to the United States and went on a spending spree that included a splashy Corvette.

Wanted posters offered a $10,000 reward for Johnston's capture, showing him in a white tuxedo and describing him as a "neat dresser, night club habitué, a Champagne drinker, enjoys female companionship." Johnston was arrested at Denver nightclub Chez Paree after 17 days, famously telling authorities, "I wondered what it would be like to have all that money. Now I know." Johnston returned the stolen cash and was sentenced to four years in prison. After early parole, he became an accountant and stayed out of trouble.

Fast forward to 2018, when a man booked lunch at Riviera, noting in the online reservation that he was bringing a friend who had robbed it when it was a bank. Johnston's group came August 10th and was treated to a tour and a visit to the bank vault-turned-wine cellar. The 85-year-old Johnston, now quietly retired, drank Champagne, shared stories and signed the brick wall with his name, date and prisoner number 5194.

After Riviera posted an Instagram photo of Johnston drinking in the wine cellar, the bank robber once dubbed the "Champagne Kid" told CBC, "Nobody understands until your freedom is taken away really what freedom is. I have such a great appreciation for life today – 60 years later – I kid you not that I would not go back to prison for any money." The wine cellar is now a private dining space, complete with the famous autograph on the wall.

Address 62 Sparks Street, Ottawa, ON K1P 5A8, +1 (613) 233-6262, www.dineriviera.com, info@dineriviera.com | Getting there O-Train to Parliament (Line 1) | Hours Tue & Wed 5–10pm, Thu–Sat 5–11pm | Tip Look for 11 carved heads of a bearded man above the arched windows of Canada's Four Corners Building, built 1870–1871. Ten are stern and one is inexplicably smiling (93 Sparks Street, www.pc.gc.ca).

94 Royal Canadian Mint
A two-word reminder of British ties

When you walk into the Royal Canadian Mint, look at what's inscribed above the arched doorway. It says simply, "Royal Mint." That's because this limestone building was constructed from 1905 to 1908 as a branch of the British Royal Mint and didn't come under the sole jurisdiction of the Government of Canada until 1931. The Royal Mint was renamed the Royal Canadian Mint, but the etching wasn't changed.

"So, for almost 30 years the Mint was essentially British – it was not a Canadian facility," explains Alexandre Reeves, senior manager of public affairs. "It became that the inscription is part of the whole heritage facility, and it has remained undisturbed to this day and will never be changed."

While the Mint in Winnipeg produces Canadian circulation coins and coins for other nations, the Ottawa branch creates collector and commemorative coins, gold bullion coins, medals and medallions. There's a boutique and guided tours that show visitors how coins are made. Look for the 2010 Vancouver Olympic and Paralympic medals on display, and tooling used to create what Guinness World Records declared the world's largest gold coin in 2007. In the gift shop, you can pose with a 400-ounce, 24-karat gold bar.

Parks Canada declared the Mint a National Historic Site in 1979. Before it opened on January 2, 1908, most Canadian coins were struck at the Royal Mint in London using gold shipped to England. The grand, two-storey building on Sussex Drive was designed by architect David Ewart in the Tudor Gothic style, with rough-stone walls, heavy and simple detailing and octagonal turrets. "The 'Royal Mint' etching," says Reeves, "is a treasured piece of history that really does speak to our origins. We take history very seriously at the mint because we preserve so much of it on our coins. That's not the kind of thing that we want to disturb."

Address 320 Sussex Drive, Ottawa, ON K1A 0G8, +1 (800) 267-1871, www.mint.ca,
reservationsottawa@mint.ca | Getting there O-Train to Rideau (Line 1) | Hours See
website | Tip The irregularly shaped, tiered Lester B. Pearson Building, home to Global
Affairs Canada, was inspired by the Great Sphinx of Giza. It's best viewed from the
southwest (125 Sussex Drive).

95 Royal Swans Plaque
All that's left of the Queen's feathered gifts

Ottawa's beloved royal swans are gone but not forgotten. In the shadow of one of the Minto Bridges (see ch. 67), lies a stone with a bronze plaque facing the Rideau River. Dated June 28, 1967, it reads, *These swans from the River Thames, near Abingdon Berkshire, the gift to the City of Ottawa of H.M. Queen Elizabeth II commemorate the centennial of the confederation of Canada.* It's a nice sentiment, the only catch being that the royal swans have been sent away, though you might luck into seeing ducks and Canada geese.

Mute swans have long been tied to the British monarchy. The Historical Society of Ottawa remembers how eight royal swans were ceremoniously released into the Rideau River just above Rideau Falls at what was then City Hall in 1967 and is now the federal John G. Diefenbaker Building. Two other pairs were originally kept for breeding purposes at the "swan house" at the city's tree nursery in the Leitrim neighbourhood. "The graceful, long-necked, white birds were an instant sensation as they cruised the Rideau River, stopping along the way to eat aquatic vegetation, as well as the odd tadpole, snail or insect," writes the society. "Couples quickly established territories along the riverbank."

During the cold Canadian winters, the swans were moved to the tree nursery, whose manager doubled as swanmaster. They multiplied, were loved by many and mistreated by others. They were joined in 1974 by two non-royal black Australian swans acquired in a swap. Some would fall prey to coyotes and other predators.

By the 1990s, the city wanted to save money on swan maintenance and reduce the flock, and critics famously dubbed the aging tree nursery "Swantanamo Bay" after the United States military prison in Cuba. The swans spent a few winters at Parc Safari in Quebec, and in 2019 City Council voted to give the five remaining swans to the Montreal-area park.

Address On Green Island, behind 111 Sussex Drive, Ottawa, ON K1N 1J1, www.historicalsocietyottawa.ca | Getting there Bus 9 to Sussex/Rideau Falls | Hours Unrestricted | Tip Enjoy a butterfly meadow and amphibian pond at the Fletcher Wildlife Garden, where the Ottawa Field-Naturalists' Club shows how to create wildlife-friendly habitats and gardens (near 865 Prince of Wales Drive, www.ofnc.ca).

96 Saigon Square
Remembering the Vietnamese Boat People

First came the statue, with a side of controversy. And then came the renamed square. The statue in bronze features a barefoot and determined Vietnamese mother running while holding a child. It was erected in 1995 in a green space at the southwest corner of Somerset and Preston that would be named Saigon Square in 2018. A trilingual sign at the base of the statue reads, *In memory of those who have lost their lives in their quest for freedom*. Saigon Square commemorates the contributions to the city by the Vietnamese refugees "who came to Ottawa in search of freedom." Using Saigon instead of Ho Chi Minh City honours the original name of the capital of South Vietnam before the country fell to the communist North in 1975.

The statue is called *Refugee Mother and Child* and is the work of Toronto sculptor Pham Thê Trung. "The bare-footed mother clutches her child in fear and determination as she escapes" Vietnamese communists in South Vietnam on April 30, 1975, explains the artist on his website. When it was unveiled, the Vietnamese Embassy was furious, and diplomats tried to stop the event. But the Federal Government held firm, and then Prime Minister Jean Chrétien sent a congratulatory message.

Between 1979 and 1980, Canada welcomed more than 60,000 refugees, who risked their lives in overcrowded, makeshift boats to escape the Communist regime in Vietnam after the Vietnam War. These people, who were trying to get to UN refugee camps in countries around Asia, were widely known as "boat people." Many drowned, but many were brought to Canada to build new lives, thanks to changes to Canada's Immigration Act to allow private groups to sponsor refugees.

Saigon Square is outside the Plant Recreation Centre between Chinatown and Little Italy. The Vietnamese Canadian Community of Ottawa still dreams of building the Vietnamese Boat People Museum nearby.

Address Southwest corner of Somerset Street W and Preston Street, Ottawa, ON K1R 7P3 | Getting there O-Train to Pimisi (Line 1), then walk 13 minutes | Hours Unrestricted | Tip The Plant Recreation Centre started as the 1924 neo-gothic Champagne Bath building before home plumbing was common. Above the entrance, look for a boy in water holding a fish (930 Somerset Street W, www.ottawa.ca).

97 Seed to Sausage's Peameal

In praise of cornmeal-crusted bacon

We call it peameal bacon, even though it's rolled in a fine, yellow cornmeal and should probably be dubbed cornmeal bacon. It's not the smoked back-bacon that Americans call "Canadian bacon." Rather, it's unsmoked back-bacon with an Ontario pedigree that hasn't caught on anywhere else in the world. Peameal is generally credited to pork baron William Davies, who moved to Toronto from England in 1854, ran the William Davies Company and built on a British tradition of rolling cured and trimmed boneless pork loins in dried and ground yellow peas to extend shelf life in the Victorian era.

Peameal usually comes thinly sliced, quickly pan-fried or grilled, and served as a breakfast dish (hello, peameal bennies), burger topping or sandwich layered in a crusty bun with mustard. At artisan meat producer Seed to Sausage, operations manager Derek MacGregor rubs centre-cut pork loins with fine sea salt and granulated sugar and lays it down to cure before rolling it in cornmeal and selling it in thin, uniform slices. The result is lean and mild with a salty-sweet edge.

MacGregor is a former restaurant chef, and while he'll admit that Rideau Hall (see ch. 92) is a peameal client, "In the scope of our production range, peameal sells well for us, but it's nowhere near our most popular item. I think there's maybe some nostalgia or tradition with peameal. It definitely perseveres."

Seed to Sausage sources hormone-free and antibiotic-free meat from animals that have been humanely raised on small farms. Unlike the big peameal producers, it doesn't inject its pork with chemicals or phosphates that bind water to the meat. The company was formed in 2011 by Mike McKenzie after serving in the Canadian military. Its production facility near Sharbot Lake has a retail shop, and there's a Seed to Sausage General Store in Ottawa, run by business partner Ross May.

Address 729 Gladstone Avenue, Ottawa, ON K1R 7B1, +1 (613) 422-5202, www.seedtosausage.ca, info@seedstosausage.ca | Getting there Bus 10 to Bronson/ Gladstone | Hours Mon–Wed 9am–6pm, Thu–Sat 10am–6pm, Sun noon–5pm | Tip Duke Fine Foods is a European gourmet grocer that caters to the Ukrainian and Russian diasporas, as well as lovers of imported goodies (2120 Robertson Road, Unit 110, https://dukefinefoods.com).

98 _Strathcona's Folly_
Unorthodox playscape inspired by ruins

One of Canada's most unusual and thought-provoking playgrounds is in Strathcona Park, where it livens up the tony Sandy Hill neighbourhood with its embassies and elite homes. _Strathcona's Folly_ is a 1992 artwork by Almonte artist and sculptor Stephen Brathwaite that looks like ruins with magnificent pillars, arches and "crumbling" walls set on an oversized sandbox. This carefully constructed children's paradise is made of concrete, stone, bronze and wood using real pieces of local architectural history.

Strathcona's Folly _is intended to encourage us to consider the cycle of life_, says a city plaque that doubles as a guide to the main pieces. There are art deco stone faces from a Bank of Montreal branch, balustrades (railings with ornamental support posts) from the Fairmont Château Laurier hotel, bronze rosettes from the Daly Building department store and an old swing seat from the park. Also look for salvaged bits of the Royal Canadian Mint, Capitol Theatre, Windsor-Duvernay Hotel, Parliament Buildings and Institut Jeanne-d'Arc, a convent on Sussex Drive.

Brathwaite, on his website, explains that the children's play area was commissioned under the city's public art program with a budget of $70,000. It "is essentially a large sand box. Like a Victorian folly, it was inspired by the floor plans of Victorian mansions that were built in the neighbourhood. It was constructed with real found stone pieces of local architectural history. Parents sit and watch over their children as they play among the artifacts of their communities past."

The design of various bronze animals – cows, bison, dogs, rabbits and others – was by Schleich Productions, most notably a bronzed rooster, the springy cartoon kind you can ride on in a playground. Look carefully for a sundial as well as two pairs of bronzed shoes set in the sand that apparently came from the artist himself.

Address Strathcona Park, 25 Range Road, Ottawa, ON K1N 8J7 | Getting there Bus 19 to Laurier E / Range | Hours Unrestricted | Tip The Rockeries contains random pieces of old Ottawa, including Soper's Fountain from Paris and Corinthian columns from Ottawa's Carnegie Library (Rockcliffe Park, www.ncc-cnn.gc.ca).

99 Supreme Court Cornerstone

Proof of the Queen's tardy arrival

Some mistakes make for good stories. The cornerstone on the southeast side of the Supreme Court of Canada building bears the wrong date. The plan was for King George VI and his wife, Queen Elizabeth, to be in Ottawa for a ceremony on May 19, 1939. But they travelled here by sea. The CBC reports that their ship was delayed by "heavy seas, dense fog and towering icebergs" and arrived two days late to Quebec City. The Ottawa portion of the royal train tour was reduced by a day and a half, and the queen laid the cornerstone on May 20 before an impressive crowd – one day late.

The country's highest tribunal is made up of nine judges, who usually wear black silk robes but sometimes slip into more ceremonial red ones. The court itself launched in a committee room in the Parliament Buildings from 1876 to 1881, and then moved to a smaller, less grand Bank Street building. This elegant grey granite building, the vision of Montreal architect Ernest Cormier, was built from 1938 to 1941 in modern classicism style with steep, château-style copper roofs and art deco elements. But the government needed to use the new space during World War II, and so the court didn't move into the space until January 1946, years after the royal visit.

"Everything is very symmetrical," says guide Talia Deslauriers during a tour. "Honestly, if you were to cut the building in half, you would have two equal parts." This observation holds true both inside and out. A Canadian flag is hoisted daily on the pole at the west side of the building, while the court's new flag flies on the eastern pole only when the court is sitting. Two statues flank the front steps, with *Veritas* (Truth) on the west side and *Ivstitia* (Justice) on the east. They're the work of Toronto artist Walter S. Allard and languished in storage from 1920 to 1970 when they were rediscovered and found a home here.

Address 301 Wellington Street, Ottawa, ON K1A 0J1, +1 (888) 551-1185, www.scc-csc.ca, reception@scc-csc.ca | Getting there O-Train to Lyon (Line 1) | Hours Unrestricted from outside | Tip Look for 13 bronze cats scattered through the windows and roof of the Dalhousie parking garage (lot 5). The 1993 *Alley Cats* sculptures are by Jean-Yves Vigneau (141 Clarence Street, www.ottawa.ca).

100 __ Thunderbird Blanket

Astronaut's gift at Canada Aviation and Space Museum

It's a Russian tradition to wrap astronauts in a blanket as soon as they emerge from their spacecraft. "Astronauts receive medical attention almost as soon as they touch down – sickness is common after landing. A warm blanket is comforting when you are not feeling well." So reads a panel for a blanket designed for astronaut Dr. Robert Thirsk by Tsimshian artist Bill Helin for the International Space Station Expedition (ISS) 20/21, on display at the Canada Aviation and Space Museum. The museum's Erin Poulton says unexpected treasures like the blanket (on loan from the CSA) can have a lasting emotional impact on the people who encounter them.

Helin, also known as Welaxum Yout, is from the Tsimshian Nation and Gitsees Tribe in British Columbia. The Canadian Space Agency (CSA) commissioned him to create a traditional Tsimshian button blanket using the Thunderbird motif he had designed for Thirsk's six-month space mission. "[Thirsk] loves Aboriginal art and wanted to culturally communicate that through his space journey, as a coastal British Columbian," Helin recalls. "The Thunderbird is the most profound mystical creature in our Tsimshian traditions, so it was fitting that Bob chose it to represent all the important elements of his mission to the [ISS]."

Helin's mother Carole, a blanket maker, applied designs and made most of the blanket, with help from his oldest daughter Reanna. Button blankets have always been an important part of Tsimshian tribal song and dance ceremonies, and Helin says his people proudly wear them. The animal designs represent clans or family members. He praised Thirsk for respecting tribal traditions and the fact that Tsimshian history dates back thousands of years. "That is why he wanted me to design a Thunderbird for his second mission crest," he remembers. "The Thunderbird came out of the heavens from another realm to reset the Earth for the next civilizations."

Address 11 Aviation Parkway, Ottawa, ON K1K 2X5, +1 (613) 991-3044, www.ingeniumcanada.org/aviation, contact@ingeniumcanada.org | Getting there Bus 25 to Aviation Museum | Hours Thu–Mon 9am–5pm | Tip Geek out on snowshoes and snowmobiles at the Canada Science and Technology Museum (1867 St. Laurent Boulevard, www.ingeniumcanada.org/scitech).

101 Tin House Court

ByWard Market's hidden lanes

In the early 20th century, second-generation tinsmith Honoré Foisy advertised his trade by decorating the outside of his Lowertown house on Guigues Avenue with sheet metal that was made to look like other building materials, such as wood and brick. Foisy covered, stamped and pressed the sheets onto rosettes, pediments, turned wood posts and other architectural details popular at that time.

When the beloved house fell into disrepair and was demolished in 1961, someone wisely saved the iconic tin façade and put it in storage for about a decade. Eventually, it was turned over to Canadian artist Art Price, who restored it with help from archival photos and pieces of other buildings. *This one-of-a-kind façade, installed here in 1973 as public art, has become the artistic focal point of this courtyard that now bears its name*, reads a National Capital Commission (NCC) plaque.

The Tin House façade, which was restored again in the early 2000s and 2016 after rusting from the effects of oxidation, now hangs on the upper stone wall of a building. The quiet courtyard also hosts the playful blue sculpture *Our Shepherds* by Montreal artist Patrick Bérubé that shows two figures, their noses connected by a long stick, standing on two blue sheep.

Tin House Court is part of the Sussex Courtyards, which run north/south between St. Patrick and George Streets just east of Sussex Drive, under the care of the NCC. The courtyards were originally the stables and backyards of historic buildings along Sussex Drive and were redeveloped into five unique pedestrian spaces. From North to South, they are called Beaux-Arts Court, Tin House Court/Maison de Fer-Blanc, Jeanne-d'Arc Court, York Court and Clarendon Court. They are all animated with art, shops and restaurant patios. Many people who visit ByWard Market's busier streets have no idea these spaces even exist.

Address Tin House Court, Ottawa, ON K1N 6Z4, +1 (613) 239-5000, www.ncc-ccn.gc.ca, info@ncc.ccn.ca | Getting there O-Train to Rideau (Line 1) | Hours Unrestricted | Tip Workshop Boutique and Flock Boutique promote ethical production and sustainable fashion, and they carry independent Canadian designers (1275 Wellington Street W, www.workshopboutique.ca).

102 — Vanier Bikers' Church

Where the motorcycle community worships

Rob McKee had never even been on a motorcycle when he was approached to be the lead pastor of Vanier Bikers' Church (VBC). But when he went for his first ride in 2016, he said to himself, "Why the heck did I not do this earlier?" Now, riding is a passion, alongside barbecuing on his smoker, making and selling rubs, skiing, coffee and the New Orleans Saints.

The VBC calls itself "a safe place for bikers and anyone else to explore what church and a relationship with Jesus are all about." On a Thursday night, scores of bikes are parked outside. Casually clad congregation members arrive early to socialize and shoot pool before the service. Having a bike isn't a prerequisite, but understanding the special focus on the motorcycle community is.

The church was established in 2002 by Garner "Hillbilly" Foster to escape a life of addiction and crime. The Capital City Bikers' Church, as it was first called, met in various spaces until landing a permanent location here in 2012. It was "planted" with support of the Pentecostal Assemblies of Canada but is a self-governing and self-directing church. It eventually merged with the Vanier Community Church and is changing its name to Vanier Bikers' Church. There's a community service Sunday mornings and a bikers' service Thursday nights (originally because Hillbilly wanted the weekend free for riding). Music – live or by video – is a big part of each service and there's a stage in the basement lounge.

During riding season, usually March or April until November, the church helps with bike-related rides, rodeos, blessings and events. They throw block parties and annual swap meets. As for McKee, while he rode Hillbilly's old chopper for two years, he now has a Harley Road King. Everyone is made to feel welcome here. And even if you don't ride motorcycles, you are sure to learn all about riding culture.

Address 156 Carillon Street, Vanier, ON K1L 5X9, +1 (613) 740-0607,
www.bikerschurch.com, info@vanierchurch.com | Getting there Bus 15 to Deschamps /
Emond | Hours Services Thu 7pm, Sun 10:30am | Tip St. Luke's Anglican Church has an
indoor labyrinth, a contemplative walking path designed on the floor of this Chinatown
landmark (760 Somerset Street W, www.stlukesottawa.ca).

103 Vanier Museopark
Making maple syrup from scratch

There are about 2,000 maple trees in the Richelieu Park forest – so many that the Vanier Museopark taps hundreds of them every spring and transforms the watery sap into maple syrup at its urban sugar shack. Sugaring-off season runs February to April, with workshops, events, school visits and a festival. Families tap trees, people learn that it takes 40 litres of sap to make one litre of syrup, and everybody feasts on syrup-infused meals of pancakes, baked beans, scrambled eggs, crispy pork rinds, potatoes, bacon and sausages. Maple taffy, made by spreading hot syrup on snow, is essential. "Thousands of people come to the property during the festival," says Madeleine Meilleur, the Museopark's interim general director. "It's very popular."

Priests known as the White Fathers, from the Society of Missionaries of Africa, once owned the land that's now the 17.5-acre Richelieu Park. They ran a scholasticate here but also built the first sugar shack in 1939 and a second, larger one in 1960. Action Vanier took over the operation and erected a new shack in 1998. It was destroyed by a 2020 fire and rebuilt yet again. The Museopark owns the current sugar shack and runs it with volunteers.

The Museopark is housed in a community centre on the site with a sugar shack mural on its façade. The non-profit community museum showcases the Francophone heritage of Vanier and the region, and its gift shop sells maple products and gift baskets. It's the only Francophone museum in Ottawa and one of few in Canada outside of Quebec. The forest has a trail called Le Sentier Des Auteurs dedicated to 30 Francophone authors, with plaques about their lives and works. Behind the public library, by a white concrete cross, look for a sealed off root cellar from 1943–1944 that the White Fathers built to hold their harvest. It's part of a decaying concrete wall near the fence to Beechwood Cemetery.

Address 300 des Pères-Blancs Avenue, Vanier, ON K1L 7L5, +1 (613) 842-9871, www.museoparc.ca, info@museoparc.ca | Getting there Bus 20 to 300 Des Pères Blancs | Hours See website for seasonal hours and events | Tip Vanier's mural trail boasts more than 30 pieces of art, mostly along Montréal Road. Look for the murals gracing Friends' Bingo (70 Montréal Road) and Hobby House (80 Montréal Road).

104_ Vanier's Grotto

Pilgrims gather at Grotte Notre-Dame-de-Lourdes

In the heart of Francophone Vanier is a grotto modelled after the one in Lourdes, France that famously draws pilgrims seeking its healing powers and apparitions of Our Lady of Lourdes (Mary, mother of Jesus). Ottawa's Grotte Notre-Dame-De-Lourdes is cared for by the Notre-Dame-de-Lourdes parish and volunteers. It's tucked into a lush, treed, fenced area on the edge of a cemetery.

"Yes, during summertime, the Grotto is an active site, where the grounds are well kept with flowers and green spaces and prayers and celebrations," explains Sister Jeannine Gauthier. "We must say that from October to April, the Grotto is an open space (day and night) with a few benches where people come to pray, to meditate and to light a candle. The devotion to Mary is visible because 'flowers' come every day at her feet."

The grotto was blessed on September 18, 1910, and a 2010 bronze plaque on a boulder celebrates the shrine's 100th anniversary. A parish pamphlet reveals that the idea for a grotto as a place of pilgrimage for Catholics dates to 1871 in the nearby village of Cyrville. There were temporary paper and snow-block grottos before this one was built on this location from stone and mortar, as well as an altar inside. The first Way of the Cross was erected in 1913, and a small store with religious objects was built in 1935. In 1993, the Grotto was turned over to the parish. When the benches are removed, the space can hold about 600 people. Look for a statue of the Immaculate Conception and a stone from Lourdes in France.

Around the site are religious scenes encased in glass, a place to light candles and two bulletin boards packed with small plaques detailing miracles and healings. A well-loved statue of Sainte Bernadette must be repainted every two years because it's touched so often. The cave is also known for drawing local cats, who stretch out among the statues.

Address 391 Montfort Street, Vanier, ON K1L 8G8, +1 (613) 741-4175, lourdesvanier@bellnet.ca | **Getting there** Bus 15, 20 to Montréal/De L'Eglise | **Hours** Unrestricted | **Tip** Admire the work of renowned Indigenous architect Douglas Cardinal, who designed the Wabano Centre for Aboriginal Health as an eye-catching, limestone-clad building with a dramatic curved front (299 Montreal Road, www.wabano.com).

105 Vintage Italian Moto Museum

A private collector's very specific passion

For decades, Joe Cotroneo methodically collected Italian motorcycles and cars, mainly buying them online out of California, dropping $500 here, $1,200 there or snapping up deals like 12 for $600. Nobody – other than select family and friends – had a clue how many he owned until he did a TV interview in the late 2010s. Motorcycle clubs and other enthusiasts clamored to see them all. In 2019, the former electrician and now owner of Pub Italia began showcasing his private collection as the Vintage Italian Moto Museum. After keeping the 158 motorcycles and 38 cars – at last count – in multiple locations, they will soon land in a purpose-built, permanent space behind the pub.

"Going back in time, nobody wanted this stuff," Joe acknowledges of his vehicles. "It's not that they're worth a lot of money – but try to find one." The moto collection includes a 1965 Moto Guzzi Dingotre, a 1953 Moto Guzzi Galetto, a 1956 Lambretta 150 cc, a 1972 Moto Guzzi Chiu, a 1962 Vespa 135 All State and a 1953 Ferrari 150 cc, among many others. On the car front, there's a 1971 Fiat 850 Spider Orangina and a 1969 Lancia Fulvia. There's even a Fiat 411R tractor. Most cannot be driven, but a select few are pulled out for special events.

Joe grew up here in Little Italy. After marrying an Irish woman, Rosemary, he opened Pub Italia in 1994, slowly snapping up surrounding properties, including the one where his collection will stay. In a recent incarnation, the collection was spread out in a series of themed rooms over the ground floor of a former dairy. People always ask him what he's going to do with his collection, which is a passion, not a money maker and possibly the largest in the world. "I don't want to think that far ahead," says Joe. "That's for my grandchildren."

Address 117 Pamilla Street, Ottawa, ON K1S 3K9, +1 (613) 232-2326, https://pubitalia.ca, pubitalia@hotmail.com | Getting there Bus 85 to Preston/Beech | Hours By private appointment only | Tip Flora Hall Brewing has reinvigorated a 1927 building that has been an electrical garage, home heating system service shop, biker garage and auto garage (37 Flora Street, www.florahallbrewing.ca).

106__ Wakefield Covered Bridge

A red beauty with a colourful past

The original Gendron Bridge was built in 1915 in the art-minded village of Wakefield, named for a federal politician and lumber merchant Ferdinand-Ambroise Gendron. The bridge first served horse-drawn buggies, farm wagons and winter sleighs. But in 1984, arsonists destroyed the bridge by pushing a gasoline-soaked car onto it and setting a fire. Nobody was ever arrested, but some blamed truck drivers angry about load restrictions and dangerous bridge conditions.

Furious and heartbroken, Wakefield's villagers quickly rallied to raise money, materials and services to rebuild. The Wakefield Covered Bridge, as it's now known, was given two coats of "bridge red" paint before it opened informally in 1987 and officially a year later, this time for pedestrians and cyclists only.

The now-iconic bridge is 87.8 metres (288 feet) long and 5.5 metres (18 feet) wide. Its walls, roof and floors are made from Douglas fir, and the exterior siding is pine. It's more than just a piece of infrastructure to walk or ride over. It has hosted hundreds of weddings and can be rented for events and activities, like yoga and performances. It's been the backdrop for countless photos.

Take time to look at the photo displays as you cross and listen to a five-minute audio history of the bridge in French or English. You'll learn that when people first settled in the Gatineau Valley in the 1800s, they built simple wooden ferries called "scows" to cross the river and get to church and stores or take grain to the grist mill. But they needed a permanent solution. By 1900, wooden bridges with metal roofs started appearing. They were nicknamed "kissing bridges" because they were dark and private.

Enjoy the black-and-white archival photo of swimmers in the 1930s and look for the flat rocks that draw sunbathers and swimmers.

Address 45 Chemin de Wakefield Heights, Wakefield, QC J0X 3G0, www.capitalgems.ca |
Getting there By car, take Autoroute 5 N, then Quebec Route 366 E, then turn right onto
Chemin de Wakefield Heights | Hours Unrestricted | Tip An 1838 flour mill powered by
MacLaren Falls was a grist mill and museum before becoming the Wakefield Mill Hotel &
Spa (60 Mill Road, Wakefield, www.wakefieldmill.com).

107__Watson's Mill

Haunted by a young bride's tragic death

Unlike most ghost stories, this one tracks to a real woman who died tragically just after her honeymoon. Ann Crosby Currier was born in Lake George, New York. On January 25, 1861, at the age of 20, she married Joseph Merrill Currier, who was twice her age and co-owned a Manotick mill. After honeymooning across the United States, they were at the mill on March 11, 1861, to celebrate its first year in business. Ann was coming down the stairs from the attic to the second floor when her crinoline hoop skirt caught in a revolving drive shaft. "She was pulled from her feet and thrown against a nearby support pillar," explains the mill's website. She was killed instantly, six weeks into married life. A heartbroken Joseph had already lost his first wife, and before her three of his four children died of scarlet fever. He sold his mill shares to his partner Moss Kent Dickinson.

Watson's Mill is a water-powered grist and flour mill built of limestone on the Rideau River in 1860 that's still operating in this village just south of Ottawa. It's the only working museum in the Ottawa area. The building actually started out as the Long Island Mill but was sold to Alexander Spratt in 1928 and then Harry Watson in 1946 who changed the name. It's now a heritage site run by Watson's Mill Manotick, which works with the City of Ottawa and Parks Canada to keep the mill functioning.

People have long reported encounters with Anne, according to the mill's Elaine Eagen. She has stared down the attic stairs, brushed against people and made her footsteps heard. The Haunted Ottawa Paranormal Society even investigated.

As for the unlucky Joseph, he married a third time, became a politician in Ottawa and ran a new sawmill in Hull, Quebec. He built a grand home at 24 Sussex Drive and called it Gorffwysfa (Welsh for "place of rest"). It's now the official residence of the prime minister.

Address 5525 Dickinson Street, Manotick, ON K4M 1A2, +1 (613) 692-6455, www.watsonsmill.com, info@watsonsmill.com | Getting there By car, take Trans-Canada Highway / Ontario 417 W to Ottawa 13 S, turn right on Dickinson Street, and the destination is on the left | Hours See website for seasonal hours | Tip The Gingerbread Man shop – in a suitably brown house with white trim – sells all kinds of cookies and baking kits (1134 Tighe Street, Manotick, www.gingerbreadman.ca).

108 _We Demand_ Mural

Canada's first gay protest

On August 28, 1971, roughly 100 people, mainly from Ottawa and Toronto, marched on Parliament Hill in the rain to present the government with a 13-page Toronto Gay Action brief titled, "We Demand." It specified 10 demands to end discrimination against homosexuals, ranging from changes to the Criminal Code and Immigration Act to human rights protections. There wasn't much of an audience beyond the RCMP and media. The impact of Canada's first civil rights demonstration for the LGBTQIA+ community and a parallel event in Vancouver would unfold slowly over the coming decades.

Almost exactly 40 years later, on August 26, 2011, people gathered at the southeast corner of Bank and Gilmour to unveil the commemorative _We Demand_ mural by Dan Metcalfe that was commissioned by the Village Committee. On the east side of the building, there's a pair of male hands holding a book that says, "We demand Canada's first demonstration for civil rights for gay, lesbian, bisexual and transgender persons. Ottawa. Saturday, August 28, 1971." A black-and-white scene shows men under a rainbow, listening as Charlie Hill reads the demands.

Hill, a member of gay rights groups who would go on to be a National Gallery of Canada curator, spoke at both events. He wasn't supposed to list the demands in 1971 but took over for speech co-writers Herb Spiers and David Newcome, saying, "All we want to do is love persons of the same sex and live our lives as we decide for ourselves." The mural unveiling was followed by a "We (Still) Demand" demonstration on Parliament Hill because there is still work to do.

A stretch of Bank Street from Nepean to James was first designated Ottawa's Village in 2011. It's home to LGBTQIA+-owned businesses, white / rainbow street signs that say, "The Village," a rainbow crosswalk at Bank and Somerset, and the Capital Pride Festival every August.

Address 365 Bank Street, Ottawa, ON K2P 1Y2, www.villagelegacy.ca | **Getting there** Bus 6, 7 to Bank/Lewis | **Hours** Unrestricted | **Tip** Stroked Ego is a go-to spot for men's underwear and socks, plus year-round Pride gear, not to mention Ottawa's largest selection of cufflinks and pocket squares (131 Bank Street, www.strokedego.ca).

109 Weird Willie's Crystal Ball

Laurier House and its 10,000+ treasures

Canada's longest serving prime minister, William Lyon Mackenzie King, was secretly a "spiritualist" who later became known as "Weird Willie." And he guided Canada as prime minister off and on from 1921 to 1948 through industrialization, the Great Depression and World War II. But the lifelong bachelor adored his crystal ball and Ouija board, and he routinely tried to commune with his dead mother Isabel through seances. King detailed these spiritual pursuits in diaries that were revealed after his death in 1950.

King lived in Laurier House, which started off as the Sandy Hill home of Sir Wilfrid Laurier, another prime minister. Lady Zoé Laurier willed it to King, and he in turn bequeathed it to the "Government and people of Canada." Parliament quickly passed the Laurier House Act in 1952 to protect the site. So, it remains frozen in time. It's now under the care of Parks Canada as Laurier House National Historic Site.

Of the 10,000 or so pieces of art, furnishings and personal effects of Laurier and King, one of the most compelling items is King's crystal ball. It's in the third-floor study, a room filled with books and dominated by a portrait of the politician's mother. According to King's online and searchable diaries with Library and Archives Canada, the prime minister received the crystal ball as a gift from A. H. Caspary, a New York investment firm owner, philanthropist and collector, in May 1937 while at London's Ritz Hotel. King had pined for it after spotting it the previous year at antiques dealer Frank Partridge & Sons but felt he couldn't afford it.

In thanking Caspary for "this perfect crystal ball," King poetically wrote that it was "as if this gift had fallen into my hands from the skies, and, indeed, from beyond the skies."

Address 335 Laurier Avenue E, Ottawa, ON K1N 6R4, +1 (613) 992-8142, www.pc.gc.ca/en/lhn-nhs/on/laurier, pc.lhnmaisonlaurier-laurierhousenhs.pc@canada.ca | **Getting there** O-Train to uOttawa (Line 1), then walk 10 minutes | **Hours** See website for seasonal hours | Tip Mackenzie King willed his Quebec retreat to Canada. Mackenzie King Estate's cottages serve as museums, ruins, gardens and a café named for the prime minister's dogs (Gatineau Park, Quebec, www.ncc-ccn.gc.ca).

110 Wellington Marbles
Fire hydrants fused with ordinary objects

You'll want to find all the Wellington Marbles that Canadian artists Marcus Jones and Ryan Lotecki created in 2010. There are 18 hand-carved marble and limestone sculptures scattered along Wellington Street West between Hampton Avenue and Spadina Avenue at Somerset Square Park. But some magically blend into the streetscape and are somehow easily missed, so it may take you a few visits to spot them all.

Each sculpture fuses a fire hydrant with an every-day object, like an artist's tool, a food, or useful object that has some connection to the surrounding neighbourhood. Wellington West is made up of two neighbourhoods: Wellington Village and Hintonburg. The sculptures were commissioned by the city as part of the Wellington Street West reconstruction project. As the city's website puts it, "The Wellington Marbles pay tribute to the local history and modern renewal of the community."

Lotecki apparently chose the fire hydrant as the unifying feature in a nod to the way that these mundane but essential objects are in every community and how they "connect people in an uncelebrated yet vital manner." When the hydrants are coupled with a second, contemporary object that culturally references the area, they become playful sculptures. The high-quality marble was quarried in Carrara, Italy and was chosen for its association with classical art.

The artists divided up the project, each creating nine of the grey-white sculptures. Lotecki focused on the sculptures of the bee and beehive, the fiddle head (the instrument, not the edible fern), SLR camera, paint brushes, artichoke, piano keyboard, car seat and teddy bear, asparagus and bell pepper. Jones sculpted the peas in a pod, corn cob, garlic bulb, gourd, paint tube, firefighter boots and hose, first generation desktop computer and mouse, top hat and draped fabric, and stack of books with an apple.

111 Yap Stone

Bank of Canada Museum's mega money

The new Bank of Canada Museum went modern and interactive in 2017, but it's a centuries-old coin from the Pacific Ocean that is the quiet star here. It's known as the Yap stone. When you enter the large pyramid that houses this subterranean museum, and start down the stairs leading to the entrance, you'll see it on a pedestal.

The mammoth stone disc with a hole in its centre is money from the Yap Islands, an archipelago of the Federated States of Micronesia. This one is rumoured to be the largest coin outside of its homeland. According to the museum, these stones (also called rai or fei) were once quarried on the island of Palau and moved 500 kilometres to Yap on perilous raft journeys before the islands switched to the much more portable US dollar. Ranging from a few centimetres to about four metres in diameter, Yap stones were usually too heavy to change hands physically, so people simply agreed to ownership changes. This one likely stood outside its owner's house before being moved to Ottawa. For decades, it stood in the garden court of the Bank of Canada's head office. Then it was put in storage for four years as the bank underwent an office renewal that included reimagining and relocating its basement museum to a dedicated space across the plaza. The free museum relaunched on Canada Day in 2017.

After you create an avatar to represent yourself in various exhibits, you can enjoy activities, like designing a personalized bank note and learning how the bank keeps inflation on target (more exciting than it sounds). "See the economy from a whole new perspective – yours," is how the museum entices its visitors. The 1,580-square-metre (17,000-square-foot) museum also houses more than 128,000 artifacts from Canada's National Currency Collection, including a prestigious 1911 silver dollar. In the Yap Islands, yap stones are commemorated today on local license plates.

Address 30 Bank Street, Ottawa, ON K1A 0G9, +1 (613) 782-8914, www.bankofcanadamuseum.ca, museum-musee@bankofcanada.ca | Getting there O-Train to Parliament (Line 1) | Hours See website | Tip Canadian music icons Blue Rodeo wrote "Stage Door" dedicated to the sketchy alley behind Barrymore's Music Hall (323 Bank Street, www.facebook.com/barrymores.ottawa).

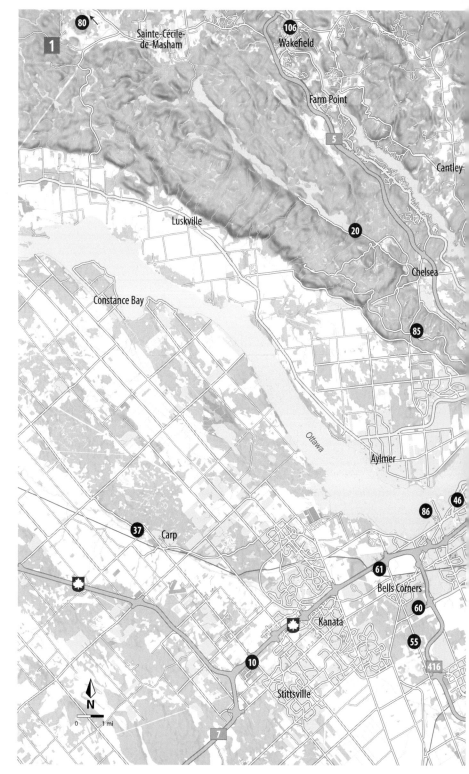

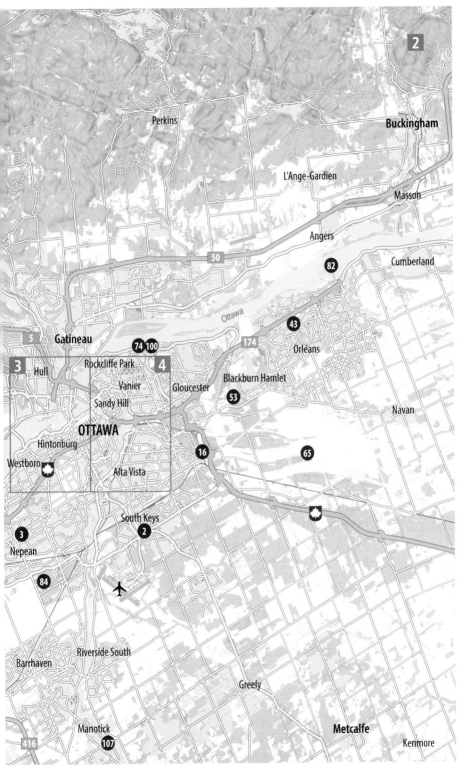

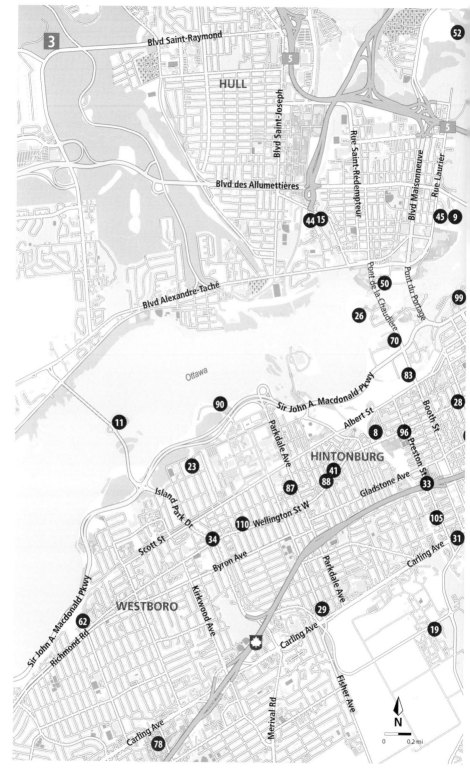

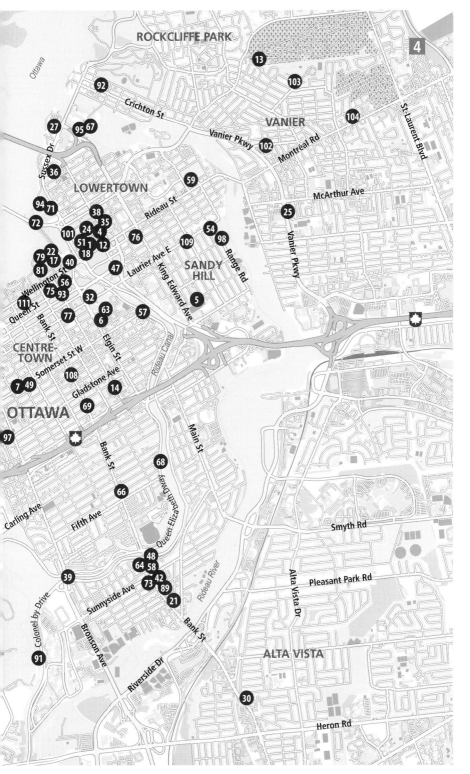

Jennifer Bain, Christina Ryan
111 Places in Calgary
That You Must Not Miss
ISBN 978-3-7408-0749-8

Elizabeth Lenell-Davies,
Anita Genua, Claire Davenport
111 Places in Toronto
That You Must Not Miss
ISBN 978-3-7408-0257-8

David Doroghy, Graeme Menzies
111 Places in Vancouver
That You Must Not Miss
ISBN 978-3-7408-0494-7

David Doroghy, Graeme Menzies
111 Places in Whistler
That You Must Not Miss
ISBN 978-3-7408-1046-7

Jo-Anne Elikann
111 Places in New York
That You Must Not Miss
ISBN 978-3-95451-052-8

Evan Levy, Rachel Mazor,
Joost Heijmenberg
111 Places for Kids in New York
That You Must Not Miss
ISBN 978-3-7408-1218-8

Andréa Seiger, John Dean
111 Places in Washington
That You Must Not Miss
ISBN 978-3-7408-1560-8

Kaitlin Calogera, Rebecca Grawl,
Cynthia Schiavetto Staliunas
111 Places in Women's
History in Washington
That You Must Not Miss
ISBN 978-3-7408-1590-5

Allison Robicelli, John Dean
111 Places in Baltimore
That You Must Not Miss
ISBN 978-3-7408-0158-8

Kim Windyka, Heather Kapplow,
Alyssa Wood
**111 Places in Boston
That You Must Not Miss**
ISBN 978-3-7408-1558-5

Amy Bizzarri, Susie Inverso
**111 Places in Chicago
That You Must Not Miss**
ISBN 978-3-7408-1030-6

Amy Bizzarri, Susie Inverso
**111 Places for Kids in Chicago
That You Must Not Miss**
ISBN 978-3-7408-0599-9

Michelle Madden, Janet McMillan
**111 Places in Milwaukee
That You Must Not Miss**
ISBN 978-3-7408-0491-6

Sandra Gurvis, Mitch Geiser
**111 Places in Columbus
That You Must Not Miss**
ISBN 978-3-7408-0600-2

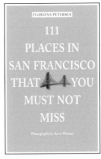

Floriana Petersen, Steve Werney
**111 Places in San Francisco
That You Must Not Miss**
ISBN 978-3-95451-609-4

Laurel Moglen, Julia Posey,
Lyudmila Zotova
**111 Places in Los Angeles
That You Must Not Miss**
ISBN 978-3-7408-0906-5

Cristyle Egitto, Jakob Takos
**111 Places in Palm Beach
That You Must Not Miss**
ISBN 978-3-7408-1452-6

Dana DuTerroil, Joni Fincham,
Daniel Jackson
**111 Places in Houston
That You Must Not Miss**
ISBN 978-3-7408-0896-9

Photo Credits

Bytown Museum (ch. 17): *Death Hand of Thomas D'Arcy McGee*, 1868, plaster, Bytown Museum, N65

Gay Sweater (ch. 45): Canadian Museum of History, photo Steven Darby, IMG 2022-0025-0001

National Gallery Stairs (ch. 72): NGC, Ottawa (top); Ottawa Tourism (bottom)

Rideau Hall's Sentries (ch. 92): Ottawa Tourism

Weird Willie's Crystal Ball (ch. 109): Juan Sanchez, Parks Canada

Yap Stone (ch. 111): Bank of Canada

Jennifer Bain Head Shot: Adrienne Amato

Liz Beddall Head Shot: Ivanka Hanley

Art Credits

The Dorothy O'Connell Monument to Anti-Poverty Activism (ch. 6): cj fleury

Lord Stanley's Gift Monument (ch. 56): Covit / Nugyen / NORR commissioned by LSMMI

Corso Italia Heritage Mural (ch. 33): Karole Marois, www.karolem.com

2020_Dis-moi ti-jos comment t'es devenu un géant (ch. 44): Sentier Culturel, Ville de Gatineau, Jean-Yves Vigneau, artist

Mōnz (ch. 68): Claude Latour

Untitled (Pimisi / Eel) (ch. 83): Nadia Myre

Refugee Mother and Child (ch. 96): Pham Thê Trung

Strathcona's Folly (ch. 98): Stephen Brathwaite

Thunderbird Blanket (ch. 100): Bill Helin

We Demand (ch. 108): Dan Metcalfe

Wellington Marbles (Corn) (ch. 110): Marcus Jones

To Jantine Van Kregten from Ottawa Tourism, nobody loves the city the way that you do. Thank you for answering all my crazy emails, thinking of me when you use a new public washroom, walking alpacas with me and pointing me in all the right directions. To Guy Thériault from Parks Canada, your colourful guided tours (first by car, then by pontoon boat) of Vanier, the Ottawa River and the city's nooks and crannies were a treat. Merci also to Eric Magnan. To Annie Léveillée from Tourisme Outaouais, thank you for sharing your love of the Quebec side of the region. To Liz Beddall, thank you for photographing the heck of your hometown, undaunted by pandemics, rain, snow and rallies. To Karen Seiger and Laura Olk from Emons Verlag, it has been a pleasure making this book with you. And to friends and family, who shared tips and cheered me on through turbulent times, I really couldn't have done it without you.
Jennifer Bain

It would be silly of me not to begin by acknowledging my friend and mentor Jennifer Bain, without whom I would not be writing these acknowledgements. Thank you for inviting me to come along with you on this incredible journey (and so many others) and for laying *all* the brickwork for this project while I simply painted the walls. An enormous thank you is owed to my sister Coo and her fam (Teelair, Anne and Jib), for housing me and feeding me (and lending me a car) throughout this process. Another goes out to my incredible parentals (Mary-Jean and Peter), to my brother Mike and his fam (Kumi and Kota), to my brother Steve and his partner Nancy, to my E. S. P. Cannon and to all my Ottawa beloveds who accompanied me on excursions, cheered me on and kept me sane throughout the last year and a half. Finally, I'm beyond grateful to the Emons team and to Karen Seiger for trusting me to take on this project. Reconnecting with my hometown has been a joy – thanks to you, and thank you Ottawa!
Liz Beddall

Jennifer Bain is an award-winning Canadian journalist who travels the world in search of quirk. She started her newspaper career in Calgary and Edmonton writing hard news before spending 18 years at Canada's biggest newspaper in Toronto as travel editor, food editor and Saucy Lady columnist. Jennifer has three kids, two cookbooks (*Buffalo Girl Cooks Bison* and the *Toronto Star Cookbook: More Than 150 Diverse & Delicious Recipes Celebrating Ontario*) and one jam-packed travel schedule as a freelance writer. Jennifer is the author of *111 Places in Calgary That You Must Not Miss*.

Liz Beddall is an Ontario-based photographer who happily splits her time between Toronto and her hometown of Ottawa. Specializing in lifestyle and documentary photography, Liz graduated from Carleton University's journalism program before embarking on a vibrant and diverse career shooting for major news outlets, lifestyle publications, established institutions and expanding businesses. She is also a writer and an avid explorer who loves the woods, rainstorms and the smell of a campfire.